"Become a 'possibilitarian'. No matter how dark things seem to be or actually are, raise your sights and see the possibilities- Always see them, for they are always there."

~ Norman Vincent Peale ~

DEDICATION

This book was written for all of humanity but there are three special people in my life who have shared me with the world. They have supported me unconditionally while I've worked hard, chasing my purpose and my dream to heal the world over the years.

This book is dedicated to them:

Mark, Laura & David
(Bubs, Loonchkie & Davie-Dave)

You are my purpose and *my* world!

This book was written for you, for us and for the world. Always know that you can be whomever you choose to be.

Shine bright and believe in yourselves.

ACKNOWLEDGEMENTS

I am the luckiest person I know.

'Life' has provided me with a plethora of challenges to learn from and experiences to grow from. My journey has been filled with many ups and its fair share of downs. I have cried tears of frustration at our bleak financial situation, felt the devastating heartbreak of loss and been challenged beyond what I thought I could handle. I have had to pull myself up from the brink of despair several times along the way, when my certainty and belief in myself were put to the test. The pressure has often felt so overwhelming I considered giving up (more than once).

But I didn't!
And that is largely thanks to the incredible people I am blessed to have in my life.

My phenomenal husband and gorgeous children.

My supportive and devoted parents who have lovingly guided me throughout my life.

My courageous sisters, Yehudit (Lee) and Caren (Ceza), I love you more than words can express and can't even begin to quantify the hours upon hours of conversations we've had about life, love, spirituality, purpose, parenting, relationships... Thank you for indulging me and for being so honest and true.

Lisa, my soul sister, who has picked me up so many times. Thank you for reminding me time and time again that my purpose is so much more than I can even begin to imagine. Your dedication to raising awareness and consciousness in the world is inspiring and I could think of no one more worthy to help me spread positivity.

Idit Ginsberg (and Maxie), my 'other-other half', my strategy partner and rock of support in all things; friendship, work, life, love, parenting... You are an inspiration to me in so many ways. Your special brand of tough love has kept me honest and steered me forward. Thank you for not giving up on me, even when I've changed direction without warning... I honestly don't know where I'd be without you holding my hand, keeping me focused and believing in me.

I am and will remain eternally grateful for the gentle encouragement and unwavering support, (and often a good old kick) to keep moving forward with this, from the special network of people I have around me.

Marilyn Messik, author, copywriter, editor (and networker) extraordinaire! You are the gentle voice sitting on my shoulder, encouraging me to get this done and making damn sure I actually do it. You have the most phenomenal way with words and a generosity that knows no bounds. I literally couldn't have done this without you.

Jo Selwyn, for joining me on this fabulous journey, for your generosity, sensitivity, honesty, love and care. Thank you for making sure we get The SMILE System™ out there into the big wide world. How lucky are we to have found one another - kindred spirits, totally aligned and in-tune in our calling and mission to help and heal others. This is only the beginning baby… !

To Adam Selwyn, for your incredible eye, clever branding and gorgeous cover design to ensure The SMILE System™ truly shines.

Your input is valued and very much appreciated.

And, Belinda Copitch for jumping on board so wholeheartedly, for being my sounding board and playing a superb devil's advocate to ensure we've considered the even bigger picture. *Brady Boy (my furbaby) loves his Aunty Belinda so, so much!*

To all the SMILE Students who have been so fully and completely open to learning the insights and teachings of this framework. I am in awe of the courage and honesty you have brought with you into this process. You inspire me to keep moving forward.

I have been lovingly supported, gently encouraged and nudged along by my incredible family and wonderful friends. Everything I am, all that I have become and everything I have learned on my journey has brought me to this point and I am overflowing with gratitude.

Thank you for believing in me so much. **X**

Copyright @2012 Ronit Gerber

All rights reserved. No part of this book may be used or reproduced by any means, graphic, electronic, or mechanical, including photocopying, recording, taping or by any information storage retrieval system without the written permission of the Publisher except in the case of brief quotations embodied in critical articles and reviews. Because of the dynamic nature of the internet, any web addresses or links contained in this book may have changed since publication and may no longer be valid. The views expressed in this work are solely those of the author and do not necessarily reflect the views of the Publisher, and the Publisher hereby disclaims any responsibility for them. The author of this book does not dispense medical advice or prescribe the use of any techniques as a form of treatment for physical, emotional, or medical problems without the advice of a physician, either directly or indirectly. This is a work of fiction. Names, characters, businesses, places, events and incidents are either the products of the author's imagination or used in a fictitious manner. Any resemblance to actual persons, living or dead, or actual events is purely coincidental.

Printed in the United Kingdom

ISDN No: 9781799192923
First Edition

Author Links:
Website: www.ronitgerber.com
Email: info@ronitgerber.com
Twitter: https://twitter.com/ronitgerber
https://www.linkedin.com/in/ronitgerber/
https://www.facebook.com/ronit.gerber

Editor's Links
Create Communication:
www.createcommunication.co.uk
https://twitter.com/marilyn_messik
www.linkedin.com/in/createcommunication/
www.facebook.com/createcommunication/
Vintage Ladies http://www.thevintageladies.co.uk/
Getting it Write - **https://tinyurl.com/yap85fhn**

Publishing Links:
SatinPublishing:
http://www.satinpublishing.co.uk
https://www.facebook.com/Satinpublishing
Email: nicky.fitzmaurice@satinpublishing.co.uk

Introduction:	- 1 -
HOW IT ALL BEGAN	- 5 -
AND NOW IT'S YOUR TURN	- 8 -
Before We Begin…	- 11 -
Introducing S.M.I.L.E	- 19 -
Chapter One	- 23 -
Laura's Story	- 26 -
The View From Here	- 28 -
ACTIVITY 1	- 32 -
ACTIVITY 2	- 36 -
Chapter 2	- 39 -
ACTIVITY 3	- 46 -
ACTIVITY 4	- 60 -
ACTIVITY 5	- 62 -
Chapter 3	- 65 -
ACTIVITY 6	- 78 -
ACTIVITY 7	- 79 -
ACTIVITY 8	80
ACTIVITY 9	- 82 -
Chapter 4	- 85 -
Chapter 5	- 103 -

ACTIVITY 10 ....- 121 -
ACTIVITY 11 ....- 123 -
CONCLUSION ....- 125 -
If Life Is A Game ....- 129 -
The SMILE System™ Core Skills ....- 139 -

Introduction:

This book has been written especially for you.

Dear Reader,

You are more than likely holding this book in your hand right now because, like me, you're on the treadmill of life, peddling like crazy trying to keep up, juggling a myriad of tasks whilst navigating the inevitable obstacles that arise along the way, asking yourself, (whenever you have a moment!) 'How on earth is it possible to keep my balance when everything is sliding downhill?' And boy can things slide!

I've been in a fair number of dark, scary and overwhelming places over the years and I know I'm not alone. Every one of us faces challenges and we all trip over unexpected obstacles as we make our way through life. Some are major challenges that whip the carpet right out from under your feet without so much as a warning word, others are minor setbacks but can be just as frustrating to deal with. Any difficult issue - big and devastating or small and irritating - makes it tough to consistently feel positive. We all have weak spots and even when you're in a good place (internally speaking) there are always buttons that can be pressed and aspects of life that can throw you totally off balance.

Whatever your circumstances, you and I have a life-changing journey ahead of us. Using The SMILE System™ as map and compass, we will explore ways to tap into a stronger part of yourself, raise your self-awareness, expand your consciousness and ultimately inspire you to lead a more authentic, balanced and fulfilled life.

The SMILE System™ will empower you to work through challenges and obstacles in a new way, to emerge more positive than ever before. I hope you'll feel inspired to take action, shift the way you view challenges, cope with turmoil and handle more easily whatever life throws at you.

Whatever situation you find yourself dealing with, now or in the future, never forget, if it's affecting you, it's important and deserves attention.

This book and The SMILE System™ is not a replacement for professional or specialised support and you might find enlisting the help of an expert in whatever challenging area you're facing would serve you well - someone who can help you see issues more clearly and formulate tailor-made practical solutions.

HOW IT ALL BEGAN

The SMILE System™ came into being in a moment of personal reflection and inspiration; it's a logical gathering of the valuable resources, tools and techniques which I've found to be extraordinarily effective over the years, to carry me safely through challenging situations. I believe its 5 key concepts have moulded me into who I am today.

At the time The System came together for me, I wasn't in a good place at all. I was in an emotional quicksand, sinking deeper into despair, stuck in a rut, utterly disillusioned and disheartened by what I saw as my lack of progress. I was angry with myself, extremely angry, because I had every reason to feel completely fulfilled and happy. I was surrounded by incredible people; a loving family, loyal friends and dedicated colleagues. Professionally, I was busier than ever with a thriving practice, a growing clinic and an impressive exhibition to top it all off. Nevertheless, I felt unfulfilled and lost. I felt I'd lost sight of every single resource I'd relied on in the past to get me through the emotions I was now experiencing.

To rub salt in the wound, many of those around me seemed down in the dumps, overwhelmed and depressed by their own life challenges. Close friends of ours were buried in massive financial debt and couldn't see a way out; my mum was struggling with bullying and nastiness at work but dependent on her job, couldn't leave; several other friends were nursing loved ones through critical illness and dealing with health crises of their own. Beyond my own circles, the wider world was experiencing economic and political turmoil, devastating natural disasters and inconceivable human destruction.

I felt there was something more I should and could be doing rather than merely going through the motions. I should be fulfilling my purpose, living life to the full and so, not being keen on sitting back and twiddling my thumbs, I started to actively re-evaluate my life and its purpose.

This was all happening back in November 2012, when I was preparing a talk to be given at a health and wellbeing exhibition. There's no doubt in my mind that the powerful, deep-rooted and unsettling emotions I was experiencing coloured and shaped my presentation in the most incredible, life-changing way.

I decided I was going to do my utmost to make the talk powerfully inspiring, not only for my audience, but for me too. I felt an extraordinarily strong need to give each and every person present, effective enabling tools. I wanted them to feel motivated, empowered and excited by their lives. I wanted them to see all they had and all they could achieve. I needed them to look towards the future, with a renewed sense of possibility and positivity. I wanted to take the positive thinking, concepts so many of us have tried and tested over the years and create a longer-lasting, simple, practical and applicable system to follow and live by.

I focused on the transformational impact I was hoping it would have on my audience. I prayed for inspiration and, as if by magic, all my coping mechanisms came pouring out in the simplest, clearest way, becoming ever more defined as I wrote. Concepts I'd internalised that had helped me strengthen my mind-set, tools I'd used successfully in the past to develop a more empowered attitude, all came alive again in my mind and slotted neatly into place in my system. I knew immediately that the only name for it could be The SMILE System™.

Over the years, so many people had told me how much they loved my positive attitude to life, no matter what I was going through. Thinking back on this wonderfully uplifting feedback made my need to reignite the drive I felt I'd lost, even stronger. And at the same time, I wanted to share it with others. All these different factors suddenly slotted together, blending beautifully to make up The SMILE System™ – a simple yet powerful process of nurturing and growing emotional resilience, the ability to bounce back and stay positive, whatever you're dealing with.

AND NOW IT'S YOUR TURN

I have been in many overwhelming situations over the years and have learned some incredible lessons, I've grown tremendously and am thankful for having been through those challenges, because, it's thanks to those that I'm able to share my story with you now. I hope you will read this book and enjoy completing the activities specially designed to help you internalise the ideas. I hope you will choose to tap into The SMILE System™ and all its resources, so you can start to truly live it and in doing so, relish being the centre of your own perfect universe, making the most of your life whatever the challenges.

Before We Begin…

Laying The Foundations

"Knowing yourself is the beginning of all wisdom."

Aristotle

Let's consider how YOU fit into the grand scheme of things . . .

Being positive begins with you!

It is therefore crucial to spend some time focusing on you and how you fit into the grand scheme of things. Let's explore a different way of seeing yourself and all you have around you.

You are the centre of your own universe. Everything and everyone around you is there FOR you.

Think of yourself as the sun of your very own solar system, sitting in the centre of everything that surrounds you, all the people, events and circumstances in your life circulating around you like planets. Each and every one is there to serve you and only you. You have drawn them towards you with your gravitational pull - your energy - the vibe of your words, feelings, thoughts and actions.

Imagine yourself as the sun, shining brightly in the centre. Picture all the people in your life surrounding you, each of them also sitting in the centre of their own solar system, which in turn revolve around you. These people, along with the events and circumstances that form part of your world, revolve around you and together make up your personal universe.

With you at the centre of your own universe you have indescribable power - to draw things towards you and likewise to release things. You see, your energy or vibe, or more simply put, your attitude to life and the way you behave, think and feel is your gravitational pull. It is this energy that has drawn towards you, all the people, circumstances and situations that you currently have in your life.

And here is the mind-blower - the eye opener that should change everything for you . . .

Situations or circumstances are what they are, life happens, *but, you can choose* the way you respond and thereby the energy you give off. It really is up to you. **Ultimately, you have the power to consciously create your very own universe through the choices you make.**

Therein lies your true power.

This concept of a person-centred solar system is not meant to sound egotistical but is a way of seeing our symbiotic existence and connection with everything and everyone in our lives whilst, at the same time, highlighting the incredible power each and every one of us possess.

This person-centred solar system exists for every single person on the planet. We are *all* centres of *our own* universes and, through our personal centres of gravity, draw people and circumstances towards us.

Taking this concept further, consider that as human beings we co-exist with those around us. Our individual solar systems intricately interconnect with other people's, making us part of *their* personal solar systems and together our solar systems combine to form larger universes which in turn interconnect and expand to form grander, more incredible galaxies. Essentially, everything is connected.

And, in the same way that astrological solar systems constantly change in response to solar forces, these person-centred solar systems or universes constantly change and evolve too - in direct response to changes made by the person in the centre.

Relating this idea to you, your universe will continuously change and evolve depending on your gravitational pull. In other words, the various things that make up your life; the people you have around you, the situations and events you experience and the challenges you face, can and will continuously change, depending on your choices, consciousness and energy, because at the end of the day, *you* are the centre of your own universe.

You have infinite power, but like most people, you probably live a life of ups and downs. You have financial, health and relationship commitments and issues as well as having to deal with those unexpected trials and tribulations life has a tendency to throw at you.

It seems to be a human condition to experience both highs and lows as we make our way through life.

The good news is you can reclaim your power! You can change the way you view and deal with challenges to create a more balanced and empowered life for yourself. You have inherent positivity skills that automatically come into play when things are going well. It's easy to think and feel positive when life is going to plan, but the truth is, no matter what you are going through, you still have that positivity within you. You simply need to know it's there and be able to locate the skills and techniques that exist within you.

Better still, you can practice thinking, feeling and acting positively until it becomes second nature. You can develop and strengthen your positive thinking muscles, so within a short time they become part of the way you live your life. When things go wrong you'll find thinking positively will inevitably make you feel more optimistic about situations and outcomes. You'll see possible solutions with more clarity, feel more able to take action and work through challenges in a proactive way.

These are the principles upon which The SMILE System™ is built. Helping you connect to the positivity within, it provides you with tools, techniques and processes, and above all, a framework for self-motivation and empowerment.

Simply knowing about The SMILE System™, will change the way you view and deal with challenges, but by further developing the positivity skills within yourself they will become a larger part of your consciousness, ensuring you can tap into them when you need to the most.

Ready to start?

Introducing S.M.I.L.E

You've probably heard people talking about *smiling through*. This is because using the muscles we use to smile is supposed to shift something in the brain, making you feel happier and more positive. **Even though it can seem pointless to pin on a grin when you least feel like it, there is in fact firm scientific evidence that this works on a physiological level.** Think about it, by deciding to smile you're telling your brain to move those muscles which give you a happy face. Your brain responds and at the same time, automatically raises the level of the happiness hormones (endorphins) circulating in your body. Consequently - and despite yourself - you *do* start to feel more cheerful.

Because it sounds too simple to be true, and in the interests of science, I had to test the theory. At first I felt ridiculous sitting there all alone with a silly smile slapped on, but sure enough, however daft I felt, I genuinely started to feel lighter, the dark clouds shifted and lifted just enough for me to see things differently and my mood changed – *wow* – how amazing that something so simple works so well.

I appreciate how painfully hard it is to force a smile when all you want to do is cry, scream, bare your teeth or bang your head against the wall. But don't take my word, try it out. If you go against your instinctive reaction in the face of a challenge, you're effectively taking control, you're making a conscious choice as to how you respond. And that is the very first step towards reclaiming your power as opposed to allowing yourself to be a victim of the situation.

But there is so much more you can do with a physical smile paving the way, lets delve deeper into the idea of using SMILE to create a happier, stronger, more positive you.

SMILE is an acronym for the 5 core skills that will empower you.

Each chapter in this book explores one of the 5 letters and its associated core skill in depth. I have also included some anecdotes, stories, activities and other bits and pieces that I hope will help you connect with each letter in a more meaningful way.

As you read through the coming chapters I hope you'll incorporate what you're reading into daily life. You might want to read through the entire book to get a sense of the whole system, or prefer to settle on one chapter at a time and work on implementing and practicing that skill before moving onto the next, it's entirely up to you and your individual preference.

However you choose to proceed, I sincerely hope you'll enjoy exploring everything The SMILE System™ has to offer and that you'll reach out, take it and make it your own to support you as you move forward in your journey through life. Above all, I hope you're inspired by who you are and what you're able to overcome and achieve. You are incredible! And, with the right tools, may you always feel empowered to make the most of your challenges and your life.

S*M*I*L*E

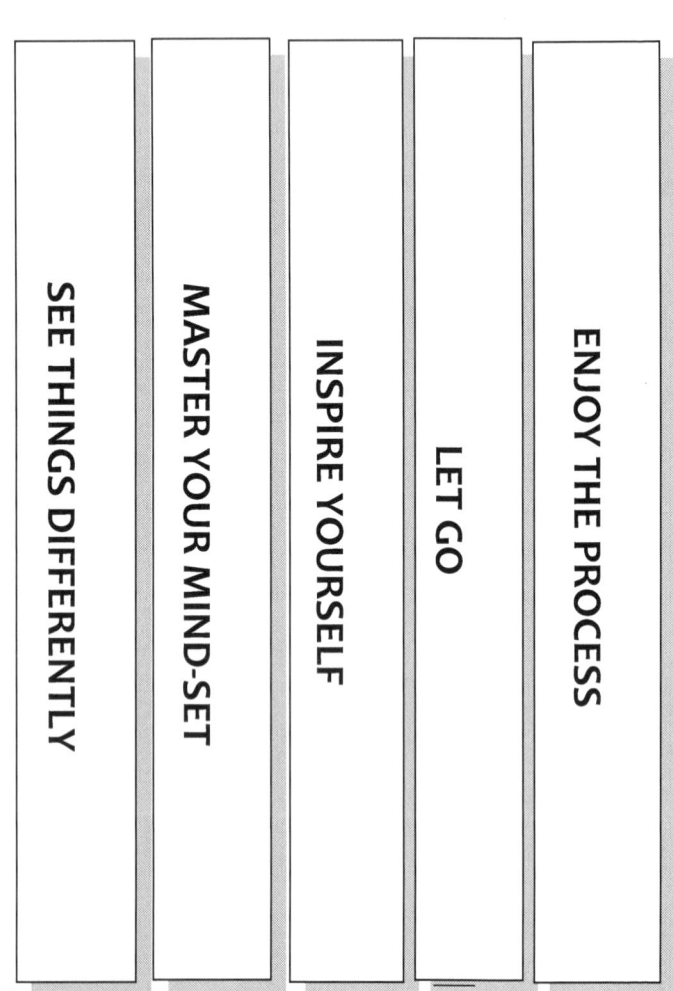

- SEE THINGS DIFFERENTLY
- MASTER YOUR MIND-SET
- INSPIRE YOURSELF
- LET GO
- ENJOY THE PROCESS

Chapter One

S
See Things Differently

"Challenges come to teach us something, to make us stronger, or to shatter our belief system about what we can and can't overcome. Once we understand the real purpose of whatever challenge we face, we will see the truth:

There are no obstacles.
Only opportunities to grow."

Yehuda Berg

It's time to see things differently!

Every obstacle you stumble upon, every challenge you experience in your life, every struggle you face, is in fact an incredibly powerful opportunity for you to learn and grow and develop.

Your challenges are your greatest gifts, the very obstacles you face contain within them your greatest opportunities. Whatever you are struggling with has a powerful and positive message for you to take from it.

Think about it, have you ever looked back at something that happened years ago, something that seemed insurmountable at the time, and thought... "OH! I get it – that's why that happened!" – "If I hadn't lost my job I never would have . . ."; "If they hadn't broken up with me . . . "; "If things hadn't gone so horribly wrong I would never have figured out that . . ."

And here's the thing... You don't have to wait to look back with hindsight to find the gift within the challenge, you can approach any and all new challenges as an *opportunity seeker*, someone open and willing to see the positive aspects of a situation in spite of the obstacles.

Ask yourself: **"As I face this situation, what are the positive reasons this is happening?"**

This requires you to be willing to see an alternative perspective, and I promise you, when you're able to do this, brilliant things will be revealed about you and the situation as you shift the negative energy around that situation into something far more positive, something that will benefit and ultimately empower you.

Think of your challenges as stepping stones towards a better, stronger, happier, healthier, more vibrant version of yourself. Each challenge you go through, when acknowledged and handled with care and intention, has the potential to teach you something about yourself and the people and circumstances surrounding you.

All too often we get so weighed down by the struggle of the challenge that we don't stop to look at and appreciate all that the situation has to offer. We don't accept or consider that there is more going on than immediately meets the eye and so we miss the opportunity for growth concealed within the challenge.

Your challenges are happening for a reason. It's your life and therefore, everything you go through is happening *for* you. I appreciate it can sometimes feel as if life is unfairly throwing all sorts of rubbish at you. But take a moment to think how unhelpful and disempowering this view is. Consider how you want to live your life - do you want to live by default, letting things happen to you, or do you make the deliberate choice to **see things differently!** Do you choose to live by design, understanding that whatever you're going through isn't *happening* to you but *for* you, for a reason, for your own good?

Laura's Story

This was inspired by an experience I had with my daughter, years ago on a family trip to Wales. She was only 3 years old at the time. We visited the petting zoo at Cardigan Island Coastal Farm Park, an idyllic place set on the cliff-edge of a mountaintop overlooking the ocean. Whilst walking around enjoying petting and hand-feeding a motley crew of animals, you have a breath-taking sea view, a gentle, salty breeze drifting up from the shore below and the sound of crashing waves and seagulls in the distance. After feeding the animals we decided to take a short hike along the cliff edge and came across a rocky alcove where there was a sign telling us we had reached the Seal Habitat. It turned out this alcove overlooks a stretch of beach where seals bask. If we climbed onto the rock formations, we would be able to look down, directly onto a beach, untouched by human hands, and have a rare opportunity to watch these fascinating creatures, in their natural habitat. At first my daughter was worried about climbing across the rocks to sit and watch the seals, but after explaining to her (in appropriate 3 year old language of course) that, without taking a chance and carefully manoeuvring onto the rocks to get a different perspective of the beach, we wouldn't be able to see them at all, she rolled up her sleeves and declared she was going to be brave . . . and she was! We sat there for ages watching the seals' playful antics as they dived expertly into the water and bounded out, flopping ceremoniously onto the sand of their own private beach. And what an incredible experience it was. I don't know if my daughter even remembers it, but I certainly do. I learned a lot that day, about choosing our perspective in spite of how we feel and the rewards of overcoming our challenges.

The following story captures the simplicity of *Seeing Things Differently* whilst at the same time illustrating the deeper benefits that this powerful practice has to offer.

I had lots of fun visualising this little story as I was creating it for you and I hope it inspires you and that it serves you well.

The View From Here

Two men are standing on a mountain top at the very edge of the summit, looking into the distance.

One of them looks down and sees a long, long drop onto the dangerous, jagged brown rocks below. He is worried about falling over the edge. He suddenly feels a gust of wind and gasps in the cold air before jumping back. He is afraid of falling. His knees go weak and he feels so shaky he has to sit down and as he does so, he looks up and sees thick white clouds scudding quickly through the sky. A shiver runs through him as he realises the wind is picking up, he is convinced a storm is on the way. He clenches his hands, closes his eyes and breathes deeply, hoping and praying his friend will say it's time to go home now.

The other gentleman looks down and sees the same jagged brown rocks. He thinks about their interesting shapes, sharp edges carved over the years by swirling waves, wind and sand. He notices the different textures on the rocks; the green moss sticking out of cracks, the slimy brown algae covering the surface and long tendrils of seaweed dancing to and fro in the water. This gentleman suddenly feels a gust of wind and gasps - inhaling deeply, filling his lungs with salty sea air. He closes his eyes before stretching his arms high above his head, and takes in another deep breath of even fresher air. When he eventually opens his eyes he looks up to the heavens. He, like his friend, sees the fluffy white clouds hurrying swiftly across the sky. A shiver of excitement runs though him as he realises he is on a mountaintop, at the edge of the world, grounded by the land but feeling he could almost reach out to touch the sky above and the ocean below. His entire being fills with awe and appreciation for everything that surrounds him.

Now, what's the difference between these two men? They are standing side by side, in the same spot on the same cliff-edge. But how they choose to perceive their surroundings couldn't be more different.

You too are in charge of your own perspective - you can choose to see a situation and take it at face value, or you can choose to look deeper and find the 'beauty' hidden within.

You can take this empowering concept a step further by *using* your challenges as stepping stones towards a better you. Explore the reasons why something is happening and look for the lessons to be learnt. Proactively seek hidden opportunity within every situation, so you can rise above the struggle it presents and transform challenges into gifts, into opportunities to improve your life. This will enable you to learn, develop and transform and you'll see that far from holding you back, your challenges will become your portal to something better.

Taking the above skill on board will serve you well, as you become someone who works through issues rather than letting them hold you back, emerging as a more confident, emotionally resilient and stronger individual every time.

This first skill, the 'S' of The SMILE System™ – SEEING THINGS DIFFERENTLY – enables you to take action, view the situation from every angle, find the pearl in the oyster and shift from the negative to the positive.

Activity 1 has been designed to help you look for the hidden gift in every situation.

(Remember to read the 'Success Tips' before you begin answering the questions to support you in getting the most out of the activity.)

ACTIVITY 1
LOOKING FOR THE GIFT IN EVERY SITUATION

1) Think about a challenge you're facing or an obstacle you feel is in your way. Is it possible you need more clarity in a certain area or are experiencing a lack in some part of your life?

~ Are you dealing with **relationship hassles?** *Does your partner push your buttons; do you have a friend who repeatedly lets you down or relatives who wind you up?*

~ Are you worried about your **health?** *Is a dodgy knee, a bad back, annoying allergies, emotional issues or other physical ailments getting in the way of you doing the things you want to?*

~ You might be experiencing **aggravation in a job** or in running **your own business**. *Does it seem as if your boss or colleagues have it in for you; are things just not going to plan?*

~ Are you weighed down by **financial worries?** *Do you feel as if you're sinking with no way out? Are you overwhelmed by bills with too much money going out and not enough coming in?*

> **SUCCESS TIP**
> It's important to approach this activity with an open mind and a willingness to put your ego aside.
>
> Accept the answers that come to you, rather than instinctively resisting them.
>
> Sit with them for a while if you need to. Internalise them and allow your answers to

2) Write down your challenge.
   Looking at the situation - Ask Yourself:

~ *What's my lesson* in this situation?
~ *How did I attract this situation* into my life?
~ *What can I do to change the outcome* and get better results?
~ *How can I transform this* into something positive?

Answering the questions in ACTIVITY 1 will help you transform all situations into something positive and beneficial. They will help you uncover the opportunities hidden in the midst of even the most negative of situations.

> **SUCCESS TIP**
>
> Action is crucial to the success of this activity.
>
> It's not enough to simply think through these questions and expect things to magically fall into place.
>
> Take responsibility for turning situations around. Gain clarity, drive and direction from these questions but most importantly - **Take Action!**

Let me rephrase, there are no negative situations (only negative ways of seeing them). What I'm saying is that even situations that feel hopeless have something vital to teach you!

By seeing the possibilities in every situation, you will be empowering yourself to create the life you want rather than being a victim of circumstances.

If you see possibility, rather than shutting down because you can't see anything beyond the challenge, you can start to take responsibility for making necessary changes.

But remember, positive thinking is never enough to turn things around, taking action is essential. By proactively figuring out the root cause of the challenge, you'll be forging upwards as opposed to sinking further at each hurdle.

Another powerful technique I often use to help me work through (and move past) my challenges is to see them as imaginary curtains concealing something spectacular. I know with absolute certainty that just beyond the challenging situation, just past the perceived obstacle I'm facing, is more happiness and fulfilment than I could ever imagine. All I need do is work through the challenge, learn from it, and overcome it, for the deeper reason I've had to endure it in the first place to inevitably be revealed. And the result is always powerful, positive and potentially life changing in the grand scheme of my life.

Activity 2 is a visualisation technique that will help you reveal the concealed and move beyond your challenge.
This technique can be used on its own or as

an add-on to Activity 1.

ACTIVITY 2
REVEALING THE CONCEALED
Try this technique for yourself.
1) Picture your obstacle or challenge as just a curtain or portal to something more, something better. See it as a doorway through which you can walk as soon as you are ready.
2) See yourself standing in front of the curtain or door which is your challenge.
3) Imagine what is waiting for you on the other side of the curtain or door - everything you'll have once you've overcome the challenge, the very thing you're striving for.
4) Now, see yourself reaching out, feel the texture of the fabric as you grasp both sides of the curtains with your hands and draw them open, first the right side, then the left. If you've visualised a door, feel the cold metal of the handle as you turn the handle and easily slide the door open.
5) Take a few minutes to adjust your vision to what is now in front of you. You have peeled open or pushed aside the obstacle or challenge so take a moment to see

what is waiting for you beyond.
6) Write down what you see, how you feel and what you now know about the challenge you are facing.

This activity will help you feel stronger, more positive, able and motivated to work through each and every challenge you are facing. You'll effectively be challenging your limiting beliefs and expectations of the situation and of yourself. This technique transforms a challenge from impossible and insurmountable into a situation that can and will be overcome to reveal benefits and positivity far greater than the perceived challenge. What's more, the determination and belief in your inner power that this technique inspires will help you work through all situations.

The two activities in this chapter work beautifully together, creating a powerful combination.

Finding the gift in every challenge by asking yourself those reflective questions in Activity 1 will help you work honestly on transforming yourself and the circumstances you're facing into something incredibly positive. And then, by choosing to see the challenge as a metaphorical curtain which you peel back, you will emerge stronger, inspired by your power to overcome everything.

I know with absolute certainty that when I've learnt what I need from a situation, when I've shifted something deep within myself or made the personal changes needed, something I have been asking for or working towards, is there waiting for me. By dealing with my challenge in the right way, I have the power to reveal the gift that is hidden behind the obstacle. And you can too.

**Greatness is not about what we achieve.
It is about what we overcome.**

Chapter 2

M

Mastering Your Mind-Set

"The primary cause of unhappiness is never the situation but the thought about it.

Be aware of the thoughts you are thinking. Separate them from the situation...

It is as it is…"

Eckhart Tolle

Are you a glass half full or half empty kind of person? Are you an optimist or a pessimist, OR, are you a closet pessimist who hides your pessimism by saying you are a realist?

Whatever category you fall into, remember that the choice is always yours!

In truth, the way we view the world around us and the situations that unfold in our lives, is directly influenced by our past experiences, our upbringing and the environment and society in which we live. We're conditioned to respond to situations in the same way those around us do. If our parents see the worst in everything it's likely we'll be wired that way too. We tend to mirror our friends' reaction to juicy gossip and shocking events in the news, adding our two cents worth to the mix. When our colleagues are outraged by changes at work it's only natural to get carried away, to join in with the moaning and to willingly jump onto the victim-mentality bandwagon with them. All these reactions send us spiralling downwards into a pit of negativity, self-pity, despair and eventually even depression. The good news is you can change these patterns of consciousness relatively easily, simply by learning how to master your mind-set.

As Albert Einstein so powerfully put it, "We cannot solve our problems with the same thinking we used when we created them." And that sums up exactly what Mastering Your Mind-set is all about. It's about **choosing** how you mentally process what's happening around you and, as a result, owning how you deal with those events and issues.

Our thoughts are a powerful part of our being. They run rampant in response to whatever is going on at any given time, triggered by our feelings at that point and fed by our own personal belief systems. Our thoughts and emotions are intricately intertwined, so interconnected that we often don't even realise that in fact they are separate entities within us. Together, our thoughts and emotions feed one another, almost egging one another on in response to what is going on around us. This inner dialogue can spiral out of control and, if left to its own devices, can eventually lead us down a path that neither serves nor benefits us.

You see, it's your inner dialogue that influences your actions and of course, it's these actions and reactions that ultimately define who you are. The way you behave, what you do, is a physical representation or manifestation of yourself. Through your actions and behaviour, you are demonstrating who you are and showing the world what you're about. Therefore, mastering how you process and deal with the myriad of thoughts flowing into and through your mind, is crucial to how you ultimately respond or react to the world around you and to your challenges.

Mastering your mind-set is the key to unlocking your potential and to staying positive despite any challenges you are facing. This is a deep, multifaceted skill with many layers. You'll find an abundance of information, books, resources and material out there dedicated to mind mastery, the power of the mind and mindfulness that you can use to enhance this skill. In truth, mastering your mind-set is crucial to your wellbeing. It's a continuous process of consciousness and awareness that will support you throughout life.

The good news is there are some simple things you can do right now to implement these life-changing skills into daily life.

Before we delve into some of the ways you can master your mind-set there is some important groundwork we need to cover so that you can truly become master of your thoughts rather than simply going through the motions.

You need to prepare yourself by getting to know yourself properly. You need to do some solid soul searching to figure out who you are, and more importantly, who you aspire to be. Reconnect with yourself. Look openly and honestly at where you are now, define who you are and what you stand for. Remind yourself of what's important to you. And don't stop there! Take it further by *re*defining who you would like to be moving forward, what kind of person do you aspire to be?

The next step is to start taking action in accordance with who you choose to become. From this moment onwards, live your life in line with the person you aspire to be. Let go of past excuses and patterns of behaviour and start making life choices and responding to situations in a way that's congruent with your new definition of self. Trust me, you'll be amazed by how swiftly you and the things around you start changing.

These two steps are deceptively simple but immensely powerful. If done with honesty and integrity they will liberate you from the shackles you've unknowingly tied around your potential. Defining yourself gives you clarity of direction and a picture of your best self to guide you. You can then act accordingly and live your life with purpose and meaning, all the while staying true to yourself.

The effect is profound and empowering beyond your wildest dreams.

Let's explore these steps in more depth . . .

DEFINE WHO YOU ARE

Defining yourself is one of the most empowering things you can do for yourself. With this simple activity you will effectively re-set your internal compass. You will be creating a filter through which you can sieve all the thoughts that run through your mind, giving you clarity to identify those thoughts that serve you best.

Redefining yourself will inevitably result in you re-evaluating everything you do right now, how you deal with things and how you relate to those around you. It will help you filter your thoughts and force you to adapt or change how you react to situations as your newly defined self.

The truth is when you know what qualities and values are important to you, your choices and responses can be made accordingly. Only when you're completely clear about the kind of person you aspire to be, can you start to live your life, make choices and deal with whatever situations you come across in a way that is authentic and true to who you are.

Let's pause for a moment to do this crucial activity.

I implore you . . . please do this one thing for yourself. This simple activity can make such a difference to how you live your life. It will help you connect to your deepest desires, to your inner strengths, your gifts and even your purpose in this world. It can then become your springboard, supporting you, guiding how you deal with any situation moving forward.

This one activity alone can change so much for you.

ACTIVITY 3
DEFINE YOURSELF BY CREATING AN 'I AM' STATEMENT

Grab a blank piece of paper and a pen so that you can jot things down as they come to you.

Create the vision of your perfect self. How do you feel, act and live your life? Let go of all limitations; the thoughts, feelings, people or situations that you feel are holding you back. You have a blank sheet, a blank canvas, and from this moment onwards can be whomever you choose.

Think about yourself in the different roles you play: as a family member; a friend; a partner; at work or in business.

Dream big and have fun . . .

If this kind of activity is difficult to do, you might find it helpful to start by taking yourself out of the equation by writing in the third person. Imagine you're writing a reference letter for yourself, or maybe a biography or even your own eulogy. Include all the things you'd want others to be saying about you.

> **SUCCESS TIP**
>
> Let go of your limiting beliefs.
>
> Imagine yourself as a blank canvas with nothing to hold you back.
>
> Think about people who inspire you, what qualities do you admire in them?
>
> Adopt these personality traits as your own, become who you aspire to be. You can be whomever you choose to be from this moment onwards…

Don't hold back. The world is your oyster and you can literally decide what kind of person you want to be in any given situation - passionate, driven, loyal, compassionate, caring, creative, vibrant, proactive, inspiring, determined, successful – you name it, you can become it!

Once you've done this and when you have a clear definition of who you are and how you want to live your life, this self-definition will underpin all you do – start living!

When you know what qualities and values are important to you,
you can make choices and respond to situations accordingly.

You'll swiftly see that although you might not always be able to change the circumstances, you can without a doubt change the way you handle them.

This brings us back to the next crucial step I mentioned earlier - Taking Action!

It's not enough to simply think about who you aspire to be. Thinking alone doesn't change anything. You need to take action. Actions speak louder than words!

By doing you become!

ACT IN ACCORDANCE WITH WHO YOU *CHOOSE* TO BE

When you know who you are, you can start behaving in a way that is true to your newly defined self. You can choose to act in accordance with who you want to be rather than giving energy to, or feeding, every thought or emotion that runs through you. This will ensure you're consciously choosing how you live your life and how you relate to people and events.

Rather than reacting haphazardly to circumstances you'll enjoy clarity of self and can respond with the truth and integrity that is congruent with who you are.

Let's explore this idea further…

When faced with a challenge we so often react on autopilot, firing on all cylinders to protect ourselves. We go into fight or flight mode to defend ourselves from whomever or whatever has 'wronged' us. Initially, these reactions feel like the right thing to do; screaming out of anger, taking revenge to teach that 'so-and-so' a lesson, doing something out of spite to punish 'them' for what they did or didn't do – these reactions can feel so powerful, almost liberating, in the moment. But here's the thing! It only feels good for that moment, because in the long run we inevitably end up feeling worse. Nine times out of ten we also end up making the situation itself worse in the process. That is because our reactive behaviour is not usually in line with who we are and how we're trying to live our lives.

Reactive responses are born out of fear, anger and the desire to protect ourselves.

They are almost always ego-driven and lead us down a disempowering slippery slope of isolation and self-doubt that eventually and inevitably make us feel worse about ourselves.

In truth things are not always as they seem at first, the full picture of a situation takes a little while to unfold. By reacting too quickly we don't give the full picture a chance to reveal itself; we are reacting without all the facts. And, when all the facts become known to us, we might end up feeling much worse than we did in the first place. Self-doubt (and even a little self-loathing) will be added to the mix of emotions we're carrying as we question ourselves, beating ourselves up, for doing whatever it is we did in that reactive moment.

To be master of your life and your mind-set you need to find a way to stop your reactive behaviour and connect to your deeper self, so you can respond from a place that serves your greater good. The quick fix of an unfiltered reaction doesn't last, it only adds salt to the wound, fuelling the fire of an already difficult situation. Often, you will end up feeling emptier, guilty or full of regret about how you reacted and, what's worse, in all likelihood you'll be left with an even bigger challenge to deal with as a result.

Not to worry though, there are some powerful tools I can hand you to help you master your mind-set, to brake before you react, to help you process what exactly is going through your mind and, most empowering of all, help you choose how to respond to your challenges in a way that will serve you rather than make you feel worse.

Before we continue, you need to be clear about who you are and who you choose to be moving forward. If you've reached this point in the book and haven't already defined yourself I invite you to pause for a moment and revisit this powerful exercise before reading further. Remember that you are the centre of your own universe. All you have around you, all that is going on in your life, is there for you, to serve you and help you be the best you can be. Your 'I Am' statement is integral to this and an essential part of your journey through the coming chapters.

When you feel ready we can move forward. Keep your newly-defined-self close, it is your inner compass and will simultaneously anchor you and lead the way as we delve even deeper into the skill of mastering your mind-set.

Mastering Your Mind-Set is about choosing how you respond to the myriad of thoughts that flow unbidden through your mind.

Mastering a mind-set is essentially about managing thoughts, or more specifically, the thoughts queuing up to come into our minds.

Thoughts arrive unfiltered, but they all have a purpose and can tell us a lot about ourselves. More often than not, our thoughts are likely to be 'attached to' or 'influenced by' our past experiences. Experiences that have contributed towards forming who we are today. But, we are more than our thoughts.

We are human beings and as such are biologically programmed to be emotional, but, we have the unique ability to think and to choose. Never forget, free-will, if used consciously and responsibly, is a wonderful gift that can help us go beyond our emotional response, beyond how we feel, to re-programme how we think and ultimately choose how we respond.

> **"Although many of us may think of ourselves as thinking creatures that feel, biologically we are feeling creatures that think."**
>
> *Jill Bolte Taylor,*
> *My Stroke of Insight: A Brain Scientist's Personal Journey*

Thoughts running through our minds trigger emotions and as humans we're emotionally charged which is why we let certain thoughts play on our minds. We mull them over and over, feed them and build elaborate stories around them, it's inevitable therefore that we also have an emotional response to these and so we spiral. How can we stop the cycle?

Here are some simple steps to help you *Master Your Mindset*:

Get to know yourself – think about your current belief systems. What limiting beliefs are you holding on to that are standing in your way? What is holding you back? How do you see yourself and your place in the world? What triggers inner positivity in you and what feeds your limiting self-beliefs?

Be honest about what's going on in your head – listen to your internal dialogue – recognise it and identify which emotions feed your thoughts and vice versa. We tend to talk ourselves into certain things and stir up emotions that don't serve us well. This awareness is a powerful way to see and appreciate that situations are not always as they seem. When faced with challenges we often inject anger, jealousy, guilt, fear or ego into the situation, making it far more challenging for ourselves.

Define who you are - Decide who you want to be in any given situation – you are not your thoughts, they are there to give you insight, they can show you which way your internal compass is pointing and help you evaluate where you are, but it is your actions that define who you are so act in accordance with who you choose to be.

Move from REACTION to CREATION - Choose to be a creator - choose to move swiftly past your instinctive, initial gut reaction and instead respond to challenges and obstacles as a creator, coming from an empowered position, knowing you can create or better yet, recreate your reality. Reaction and Creation, two words comprised of the same letters. How you decide to arrange them makes all the difference!

And some quotes and insights to inspire you:

"As you think, so shall you become."
Bruce Lee, world renowned martial artist.

Filter your thoughts, choose to dwell only on the thoughts that serve you and let go of those that don't. Thoughts create your reality so be careful what you think about! Choose to be the person you aspire to be – tell yourself you are that person – direct your thoughts rather than be directed by them.

"Unfortunately, as a society, we do not teach our children that they need to tend carefully the garden of their minds. Without structure, censorship, or discipline, our thoughts run rampant on automatic. Because we have not learned how to more carefully manage what goes on inside our brains, we remain vulnerable..." Jill Bolte Taylor, a neuroscientist, stroke survivor and author describes the importance of our state of mind in what can often be a hectic and chaotic life in the most incredible way, she says: **"To experience peace does not mean that your life is always blissful. It means that you are capable of tapping into a blissful state of mind amidst the normal chaos of a hectic life."**

Jill Bolte Taylor, My Stroke of Insight: A Brain Scientist's Personal Journey.

In other words, you can challenge your own thoughts, question them and decide to turn them into something positive ... if you can do that you are effectively training yourself to see the world through rose tinted glasses.

"I am not what happened to me, I am what I choose to become."

Carl Jung, renowned psychiatrist and psychoanalyst, founder of analytical psychology.

The only free will we have is our attitude when faced with certain circumstances.

So, how can you change your attitude when faced with a challenging situation – how can you remain positive and strong when all you want to do is scream and crumble?

How can you master your mind set and change your thoughts, actions and emotions so they empower instead of limit you? What can you do to reprogramme your behaviours and act in accordance with who you aspire to be?

Firstly, we need to look at and understand our inner dialogue in a little more depth. And then we need to find a way to replace the old conditioning with positive thoughts and empowering beliefs.

What we say to ourselves on a continual basis (self-talk) affects what and how we think and feel about ourselves. It is said that we are our own worst critics, and this is often all too evident in the things we say to ourselves every day:

"Ugh... I didn't bring my keys again today, I am so forgetful!"

"Nobody agreed with my suggestion, I'm a lousy and boring speaker, I probably shouldn't bother speaking at all next time."

"She didn't respond to any of the messages, she doesn't like me very much. Am I not good enough for her?"

Sooner or later, this negative self-talk creeps quietly into our subconscious mind so we repeat it over and over on autopilot without realizing, and worse, we allow the accompanying limiting thoughts such as forgetful, no good at speaking, unattractive, too fat, not good enough, stupid – I could go on, but you get the picture – to form beliefs which in turn influence our reality.

Thinking this way means that as you face more situations and challenges, these limiting beliefs are fed and reinforced, putting you on a downward spiral.
How can you effectively break this cycle?

MANAGING THE BATTLE WITHIN

There is an old Cherokee proverb that illustrates this internal battle of wills beautifully…

A young Cherokee boy said to his father, "Father, I feel as if I have two wolves battling inside of me. One is kind and gentle, encouraging me to believe in myself, to be generous, kind, compassionate, happy, loving and confident. He feels good. The other wolf is loud and forceful. He is telling me I'm not good enough. He is telling me to be fearful, anxious, angry, jealous and frustrated. He makes me feel bad. Father, which wolf will win?" His father wisely replied, "Whichever wolf you feed my son".

There's not one of us who doesn't have this internal battle going on. At times, when we're able to stop ourselves from reacting to situations, our wiser-self prevails. But, when things are going wrong, our 'harder self' shouts louder and more forcefully, making it difficult to hear our kinder inner voice. The 'harder self' is almost self-sabotaging in its attempt to protect us from perceived danger. It will remind us of past mistakes, limited self-beliefs and feelings of inadequacy, unwittingly sabotaging happiness. And it's always so much easier to hear the harder self. It has a louder voice and a lifetime of information with which to hold you back!

Mastering Your Mindset starts with knowing that you are more than your thoughts.

By acknowledging this internal battle taking place within you, and then deliberately and actively tuning-in to what your kinder, higher self is saying you can connect to your inner wisdom and allow that to guide your actions.

ACTIVITY 4
HEARING YOUR TWO VOICES

1) Think of a scenario that triggers your reactive nature, perhaps you have,
- Lost your way and are now running very, very late . . .
- Messed up a piece of work so have to start again . . .
- Mixed the washing and now your white trousers are pink.
- Forgotten to buy an ingredient, so can't make the planned meal.

2) How does that make you feel?

_____
_____
_____
_____

3) What is your 'harder self' telling you?

_____
_____
_____
_____

4) What would your kinder self say?

_____
_____
_____
_____

5) Which voice do you listen to?

_____
_____
_____

SUCCESS TIP

a) Pick an example that really pushes your buttons.

b) Be as open and honest as you can about the feelings it evokes in you and what your inner dialogue tells you.

USE THIS TECHNIQUE TO STOP YOUR REACTIVE BEHAVIOUR

c) The next time you catch yourself reacting to a challenging situation, use this technique to stop yourself before you react so that you can deal with it as a creator rather than a reactor.

ACTIVITY 5
NEUTRALISING INNER CHATTER - AFFIRMATIONS

Positive affirmations offer a powerful technique to neutralise negative inner chatter and in the long run, replace negative self-talk and limiting thoughts with empowering, loving thoughts that will open your mind to possibilities and opportunities instead of obstacles.

Repeat your affirmations daily, saying them out aloud, with positivity and conviction.

Here are a few affirmation starters to get you started…

I am more than enough!

I can. I will. End of story. (@dailyburn)

I am strong, vibrant, filled with hope and achieve all I set out to do.

My ability to conquer my challenges is limitless; my potential to succeed is infinite.

Everything that is happening now is happening for my ultimate good.

I am in charge of how I feel and today I am choosing happiness. (@sequellife_bp)

During your challenges you can decide who you want to be, what sort of person you want to be, and once you've made that decision you can then commit to acting in accordance.

Mastering your mind-set is about choosing – deciding – to be positive in spite of what's going on. Choosing to see the glass as half full, choosing to see the world through rose-tinted-glasses. This choice will enable you to be solution-focused. If you choose to see the worst in every situation you close yourself off from possibilities and solutions before you've even managed to find them or figure them out.

Mastering your mind-set and choosing to be positive will help you work through every situation.

Chapter 3

I

Inspire Yourself

"The creative spirit when awakened is much more than an occasional insight. It is the ability to regularly and consistently solve day-to-day problems in an innovative and unique way. It means going beyond the routine and conventional. It means tapping into the inspiration that is forever within us, flowing with ideas."

John Kehoe

"Go within and you will never go without"

Anonymous

Inspiration is the fuel that moves us and propels us forward.

Think about how alive and driven you feel when something inspires or excites you? It can be something small, an idea filled with possibilities, a poem that reminds you of something beautiful, creating something that fills you with hope or maybe being around someone who has succeeded against all odds.

Inspiration brings a positive energy with tremendous benefits, especially when we are feeling stuck, overwhelmed or despondent. The feelings of happiness and possibility it evokes and the actions it inspires us to take are immensely powerful. And here's the thing - You don't have to wait around for inspiration to come to you. *You can run towards it!*

By choosing to actively seek or plug-in to what inspires you whenever you need to, you'll be proactively lighting the powerful spark of inspirational energy within yourself. Think about how people express themselves when they're excited about something. Their eyes light up as, with beaming faces, they describe feeling "fired up". You can almost see the 'fire in their belly' as the inspirational energy fills them and they are motivated to take action, do something concrete to connect to the positive energy packaged within whatever it is that inspires them. In that moment of inspiration, it's as if they are happier, more vibrant and alive with this incredible light shining from within, driving them forwards.

So, if inspirational energy gives such an incredible boost, why not use this source of positive energy to help us when we need it the most? When we're facing challenges and are feeling stuck, defeated and low?

Whatever it is that fills you with hope, excites or inspires you, has the power to move you forward. Inspiration is an activator.

Whatever your inspiration looks like, it contains a positive energy within it that can pull you out of the darkness, out of the depths of despair and heaviness brought on by your challenges. By actively choosing to *inspire yourself* you are activating an emotional propeller that can't help but move you forward.

But it does seem contradictory doesn't it? In that moment of struggle, when things are going wrong, when everything feels as if it's falling apart, having to stop and change focus can feel like an unwelcome or unnecessary distraction.

Everyone deals with challenging situations in their own way . . .

I become obsessive. My problem consumes me. I become so focused on working out what to do that I hold onto my challenge tightly as I try desperately to sort it out. I keep going at it from every angle until it's resolved. Even when a solution keeps evading me and I feel as if I'm banging my head against a brick wall, I just keep on. And nothing changes! Apart from the inevitable detrimental effect my obsession has on other areas of my life. This is not a great way of dealing with challenge.

Of course, there are many people who, faced with an equally challenging issue, do the complete opposite. They bury their heads in the sand, pretend nothing is wrong and convince themselves that whilst they look the other way, everything will work itself out. But as they are not proactively doing anything to change the situation or the way they look at it, things continue to spiral out of control. And that's as unhelpful as obsessing.

However you respond when things go wrong, whatever you do to protect yourself from the pain you think is connected to the challenge, be aware, as human beings we can get so caught up in the *fight* surrounding the situation that the very solution we're searching for remains obstinately out of sight, masked by the struggle. Unless we change something, shift our focus to allow some positivity in, even for a short while, the best way forward will continue to elude us.

Therein lies the true value and immense power of inspiration!

By doing something creative or inspirational you are creating an opportunity for yourself to plug into something different, something that by its very definition injects positive energy into your life. Inspiration moves you from a place of lack, challenge and difficulty to a place of positivity, energy and creativity. By giving yourself the chance to connect to something vibrant and invigorating you are creating a space within yourself and opening up to allow solutions and answers to enter.

Think of it this way; when we're struggling with something or feeling in despair it's as if we shut down. We disconnect from all around us and build a surrounding protective wall. This wall prevents us from seeing beyond what we're struggling with and at the same time blocks anything from reaching us.

Imagine now you're standing in front of your *Obstacle Wall*.

It is solid, strong and unyielding. You push hard to try and move it but feel you don't have any energy left. Of course, from time to time you're forced to take a break from pushing to attend to other things in your life, but your challenge still takes up head-space because you simply can't stop thinking about it. And before long you're back at the wall, straining to push past because you hope that just beyond is a solution. But that wretched wall is so solid and immovable you can't find your way over, under, round or through. Your challenging situation is the very thing blocking you from the solution.

By turning your attention away from your *Obstacle Wall* to connect to your creative spirit, by actively choosing to tap into your inspirational energy and all it encompasses, you'll be able to re-focus on your wall with fresh eyes and renewed energy. The positivity and light you'll have awakened within yourself will help you see things differently. You'll see things you'd previously overlooked; cracks and openings will become visible to you. You'll be able to see glimmers of light shining through from the other side and soon enough you'll be able to see right through to the other side, where your solution is waiting.

As Norman Vincent Peale accurately stated, "Every problem has in it the seeds of its own solution".

Let's summarise this powerful lesson . . .

Energy surrounds us, it's in everything we do, it doesn't go away, and it can't be destroyed. It simply changes form.

Positivity is a type of energy.

When things go wrong, it's easy to feel unplugged or disconnected from positivity. But that uplifting energy is still there, it doesn't disappear, it's all around, you just need to reconnect.

By choosing to inspire yourself, that's exactly what you're doing, it's like turning on a switch and allowing light to flow into what would otherwise remain a negative, disconnected space. This not only helps you see things more clearly but makes finding solutions so much easier.

Energy you create within yourself through inspiration will light your way.

It's time to get excited! And Inspired!

We've seen why *inspiring yourself* is such an important step, helping you stay positive, especially when things are falling apart. Let's now explore how to waken that inspiration.

The first question to ask yourself is:
***What* inspires you?**

Now plug into that, remind yourself what moves and excites you – songs, poems, scenery, miracle stories, people, biographies, films – anything that reconnects you to a more positive aspect of yourself and of life. This will awaken the spark of inspiration within you as you focus on something positive and uplifting.

The second question to ask yourself is:
Why does it inspire you?

Figure out your why: When you know why and can acknowledge and enjoy the feelings you get, you can use this new awareness and boost of energy to stay positive and move forward.

The third question to ask yourself is:
What can you do to *get* inspired?

Take inspired action: It's not enough to just think about what inspires you, taking this skill to the next level is crucial to its success. The initial idea will fill you with excitement, the vision of the end result will be incredibly motivating, but if you don't take some sort of action to manifest the idea, you'll feel disappointed and frustrated. Commit to doing something concrete and do it. You will feel the benefits immediately and can utilise this positive energy to help you work through your challenges.

And there's more…

Inject enthusiasm into what you are doing: Enthusiasm is the gateway to massive, positive energy. You can choose to be enthusiastic - so, choose it - live and breathe enthusiasm (even when it seems everything around you is negative). Ask yourself, "How can I live and express enthusiasm right now?" When you choose enthusiasm, you align with positive energy *instantly*!

Surround yourself with inspiring people: Spend more time with people who exemplify what you are striving towards, people who are living examples of who you aspire to be and who are living their lives in line with the way you'd like to live yours. Look at who you hang around with. There will be people you're obliged to spend time with who leave you feeling drained and negative. But there will also be people who boost your energy, who help you feel energised and excited. Check who you're spending most of your time with. Make sure to tip the scale in the right direction, so you spend more time with the positives - people who lift you up rather than drag you down. This will help you stay strong, positive and open to all that is possible.

Adopt an attitude of gratitude: Shine the spotlight on your haves rather than your have-nots. Each one of us has something to be thankful for. We spend so much of our time thinking about what's lacking in our lives, comparing ourselves to others and wanting what we *think* they have because we believe it will make us happy. The truth is, this only serves to further highlight what we don't have and leads us down a slippery slope to even more lack. Instead, focus on what you *do have*, count your blessings and be thankful. Being grateful and appreciative of what you do have will help you feel prosperous and abundant which will in turn create an opening for more abundance and prosperity to flow in.

Find inspiration within: Be inspired by *you* and who you are. All too often we compare ourselves to others; seeing the best in them, but the worst in ourselves. We benchmark ourselves according to what others have achieved rather than looking at what we, with our own life story, have managed to achieve

and continue to accomplish. We put others on a pedestal and strive to be more like them. But we have our own journey. For one person, getting out of bed in the morning is a major achievement whilst for another, running a marathon or climbing Mount Everest is an equally major achievement. For some, signing a new business deal fills them with pride while for others, managing to save a little money every month feels exhilarating and fills them with pride. It can be soul destroying to compare ourselves to others. There's so much you've already done which can inspire you. What traits do you have that make you special? What unique gifts and qualities do you bring to share with others?
It's incredibly powerful to seek and acknowledge these gifts within yourself.

Leave self-doubts aside, take your critical self out of your own way, let your kinder-self speak. Try and see yourself as others see you, the best of you. What have you managed to do that you didn't think you could? Look within and acknowledge your own accomplishments, no matter how small. There are things you have achieved, done or created that in themselves are inspiring. Feeling inspired by your potential cannot be taken away. It's something you can carry with you wherever you are and take into whatever you are doing – look within and you will never go without.

Remember your dreams: Dreams are important for so many reasons. They give us something to look to, even when times are difficult. If you have a rough day at work, you can close your eyes and picture your dreams. You can rise above short-term setbacks because you know you have long-term success to look forward to. Not only do dreams, ambitions and aspirations help you deal with failure, they also constantly motivate you. Even if you fall short of your ultimate goal for the time being, you can still advance. Take time to think about your dreams. This may be a totally new experience for you, and if so, enjoy yourself. Think big, and don't worry about how or if it will happen. Let the excitement take over. Everyone needs a dream - it's time to create yours.

Here are a few dedicated activities to help you *inspire yourself* . . .

ACTIVITY 6

GET EXCITED

No matter what you're doing today, whether it's washing dishes, folding laundry, sending an email, making a phone call, meeting with a client or doing something you absolutely hate, try doing it with excitement. When you get excited you'll automatically connect to the positivity available in that situation. And, when it comes to the things you hate doing, excitement will help you break free of your comfort zone, empowering you to rise above self-imposed limitations and move into the realm of being able to make the impossible possible.

Inspired by
Yehuda Berg's Daily Blog

ACTIVITY 7
APPRECIATION - COUNT YOUR BLESSINGS

Appreciate the darkness, appreciate where you've fallen, and appreciate when you're low. Know that it's from those dark places you're going to reveal your full potential and experience your most fulfilled self. Start to love what you have rather than longing for what you don't, that way you won't feel in need.

Start each day with gratitude . . . **Today I am grateful for . . .**

"Go within and you will never go without" - first and foremost look at yourself and your life and find inspiration there. Rather than focusing on your lack, on the things you've lost or don't yet have, concentrate on all you have accomplished, your blessings, the things you do have and for which you're thankful. This is about appreciation and gratitude, two powerful words that connect you to your blessings and plug you into inspiration from within. This is the quickest and most effective way to inspire yourself and shift your focus to positivity.

> **SUCCESS TIP**
>
> Use this inspiring quote as a prompt:
>
> *"Count your blessings and your problems; if your problems outnumber your blessings, count again, chances are the things you take for granted were not added."*

ACTIVITY 8
FIND YOUR PURPOSE

No two people are the same, we each have unique gifts to share with the world. We each have a reason for being, a purpose for being alive. Work out your purpose. Give yourself a reason for doing what you do and use that to inspire your life.

When you're living your purpose, everything you do will be filled with inspiration. You'll know absolutely, beyond doubt, that what you're going through right now has a higher purpose. So, spend some time working out your purpose and commit to doing something each day that brings you closer to fulfilling your purpose.

"When you find your purpose, it is like your heart has been set alight with passion"

Rhonda Byrne, Author of The Secret.

SUCCESS TIP

Finding your purpose will help you lead a life of purpose and meaning. It will give you something worthwhile to draw on as you journey through life.

Take time to work out what you can offer the world.

ACTIVITY 9
CHOOSE TO BE HAPPY

Happiness is a state of mind not a destination.

Anne Frank, whilst sitting in her bedroom, living through the horrors of the Holocaust, wrote:

"Today I choose to be happy".

Think about that. Make the decision to be happy, today.

SUCCESS TIP

Action is crucial to the success of this activity ...

Finish this sentence:

"Today, I choose to be happy about . . .

_____"

HARNESS THE POWER OF IMAGINATION TO INSPIRE YOU

In his bestselling book, *Think and Grow Rich*, *Napoleon Hill* wrote, "You will never have a definite purpose in life; you will never have self-confidence; you will never have initiative and leadership unless you first create these qualities in your imagination and see yourself in possession of them." He goes on to say that, "... imagination is the most marvellous, miraculous, inconceivably powerful force the world has ever known."

Your imagination is the seed of all your achievements. An image in your mind is the first stage of the creative process in life, from your imagination your visions and plans arise.

Think about it. Not that long ago the idea of walking on the moon, communicating by email, traveling on jets, talking on cellular phones, video-calling and internet banking were sheer fantasy. Today, they are commonplace. How? Because, someone with a crazy imagination and a lot of determination had a dream, a vision they conceived and then went on to create. These pioneers used their mental faculties to fantasize, to build wild and wonderful pictures in their mind that have brought us the thousands of modern conveniences we enjoy today. They seemed to have had an innate awareness that if they could visualize it, they could do it.

Thinking of this, let *your* mind play, fantasize, build a picture of your future. There are no borders or limits on what can be built in your imagination. You can *be*, *have* or *do* anything your heart desires, anything!

To summarise, when you feel *so* inspired by an idea or prospective outcome that you're compelled to act, *that's* Inspired Action and this underpins everything, fuelling it with positivity and infinite possibility.

And you can *Choose* to get inspired each and every day!

Remember, when we feel inspired we get excited, so, by inspiring yourself, you will effectively be injecting excitement into anything you do which ultimately transforms it into a source of joy and fulfilment.

It is up to you to take what inspires you and make something of it. Or, better yet, take whatever you're doing and let it inspire you!

Chapter 4

L

Let Go

"Peace is the result of retraining your mind to process life as it is rather than as you think it should be."

Wayne W Dyer

Letting go is incredibly liberating. It creates space in our lives for positivity to enter, freeing us from the things that don't serve us so we can take hold of the things that do, in order to move forward.

One of my all-time favourite stories brings exquisite clarity to this concept - it's the one about a monkey refusing to let go . . .

A cheeky monkey stuck his hand into a glass jar to grab a handful of peanuts sitting at the bottom. After scooping up a generous helping of the delicious treat the monkey found himself trapped, unable to remove his clenched fist from the jar. Refusing to release his hold on the peanuts, the monkey remained captive to the jar.

Rather than letting go of the peanuts and freeing himself from the confines of the jar, the monkey was so invested in holding on to his treasure, he overlooked the bigger price he was paying. He was so fixated on the quick fix of the initial gain (yummy peanuts) he simply didn't consider the long- term consequences of such a choice (losing his freedom).

We aren't that different from the monkey when you think about it. We too are inherently resistant to letting go!

Why is it that even when we know something isn't good for us we find it incredibly difficult to let go?

We hold onto all sorts of things; physical things, objects we own; designer clothes, shoes, bags, jewellery, mobile phones, iPads, cars, gadgets - all the material wealth that feeds our ego, because having them makes us feel successful.

And then there are the deeper things we can't (or rather choose not to?) let go of, the intangibles, the 'stuff' that feeds our egos even more than our physical belongings; pride, guilt, anger and frustration, self-limiting beliefs, addictions, toxic relationships, destructive habits.

We hold onto these behaviours, emotions and belief systems because we've let them define us, we see them as part of our identity. And, letting go of them might feel as if we are losing a part of ourselves.

These two simple words roll so easily off the tongue... "Let" and "Go". And yet, they are the hardest to action. Looking at their meaning in a little more depth gives us a clue as to why.

To let something go literally means to allow (let) it to leave (go). The thought of allowing something or someone to leave fills us with fear. We are afraid of losing what we have or losing out because we don't have it any longer. We are worried that without that thing, that person or that way of doing something, we will have or be less than we are with it, even if it is hurting us.

What we don't realise is that by holding on to our 'stuff', by squeezing it tightly within us, not only are we keeping things that aren't necessarily good for us firmly locked into our lives, we are actually restricting the flow of new, positive energy and opportunities. The baggage we carry around with us takes up space in our lives, physically and energetically and unless we can release it when we need to, it will remain firmly in place, keeping us stuck exactly where we are.

I learned the true value of letting go in a very unexpected way when my son was born...

For years I had been 'stuck' in an all-consuming friendship. I became so dedicated and devoted to that one friend that I blindly believed she epitomised what true friendship was all about. I sacrificed so much for her. She came first, above and beyond anyone else. Other friends and family members were relegated to the bottom of my list of priorities and unsurprisingly, after a while, my list started dwindling as some very special people began pulling away.

And then, when my son was born something changed, and she withdrew in the most callous of ways. During one of my most intense, overwhelmingly emotional, life changing moments, when I was at my most vulnerable and needed her friendship and support the most, she wrote me a note and unceremoniously walked away from our friendship. Just like that!

It was painful and confusing. I couldn't understand why she was rejecting my friendship after I had placed her on such a pedestal, in a position in my life above all my other friends, and even my family. I felt utterly heartbroken, betrayed and devastated.

Looking back now, I remember all I longed for was to be surrounded by people who loved and cared for me as much as I did for them. I desperately wanted mutually supportive friends; people who would help me live my life in a balanced way. And, looking around me at the help and support I *had* received from everyone around me, it hit me that I had just that! So many people *had* rallied round, apart from that one friend I'd valued so much, up there on her pedestal. She didn't call, she didn't help, she didn't visit she was, as they say, conspicuous by her absence.

But her decision to walk away was in fact exactly what I needed at that point in time, maybe I was already subconsciously aware of that, and because she walked away, many other wonderful, inspiring, supportive friends were able to step into her place. They helped me rebalance my life and they help me still, keeping me grounded and focused on what is genuinely important – my family, my goals, my dreams and aspirations for the future. I no longer drop everything to be at the beck and call of my friends *(they wouldn't let me).*

My desire to change something in my life gave me what was needed, and I let go of a toxic relationship.

It didn't look or feel at all how I expected, but as so often happens, I couldn't see the full picture at the time. It's only now, with the gift of hindsight that I can see just how consumed I was by that one relationship and how much energy and focus it was taking from my life. By releasing it I was able to welcome in so much more. Had I known this beforehand I wouldn't have suffered for so long, I wouldn't have agonised over why I wasn't good enough for that one person nor beat myself up for what I might have done to push her away, I could have saved myself a lot of heartache.

I guess the lesson here is knowing that the process of getting from where you are now to whatever it is you're striving towards is never easy. In committing to shift or change an aspect of yourself or your life, there will be things you need to let go of to create the space for new 'gift/s' to enter.

Ultimately, when executed in the right way, Letting Go will leave you feeling freer, releasing you from self-imposed pain and suffering we so often become attached to as we move through life.

Letting go is a hugely important part of the process of becoming the best version of yourself.

But, make no mistake, letting go is tricky - there are many layers involved. It needs to be done in balance, so we remain grounded, responsible and proactive whilst simultaneously releasing our hold enough to allow creative, divine energy to flow in. Show up, do your bit, but also allow things to unfold as they need to.

HOW TO LET GO...
Letting Go sounds so simple but is one of the hardest things to do. Just because we've figured out WHAT we need to let go of doesn't mean we actually know HOW.

Here are some insights to be aware of when working on Letting Go:

YOUR EGO - plays a big part in stopping you from letting go, it is the voice within (your Harder Self) that tries to talk you out of change, stops you being honest with yourself. Your ego doesn't want you to let go. Its instinct is to protect you from perceived threats. Your ego believes that if you let something go, you'll be losing out. Fear drives our ego, so be aware if you're self-sabotaging. Tune in to your Kinder Self which will give you the inner strength to do what you need to for your own good.

TRUST - is the antidote for your ego. Trust connects you to your Kinder Self. By trusting there is a greater force out there, by believing everything happens for a reason, for your own good, you can turn down the volume of your ego. Once you've done that you'll find that so much of what you are holding on to isn't helping you one little bit.

FORGIVENESS - is another tool you can use. Practise saying to yourself "I'm big enough to make mistakes." This will take you a good way towards learning to let go.

FORGIVENESS – TRUST – EFFORT

Trust and forgiveness are intrinsic elements to letting go in the right way, in balance, so that rather than resisting, forcing or 'pushing against' the very thing you are trying to let go of, you are releasing it in a healthy and beneficial way. As Carl Jung so brilliantly put it, "What you resist persists" – letting go is not about resistance – if you try too hard to push something away it will remain steadfastly in place and worse, it will increase in strength. Fighting against fear or rejecting it will lead to more fear because you're not dealing with it effectively. Allow yourself time to process your feelings and find a way to deal with them so releasing what you need to is made easier.

Let's go back to the analogy of the 'Obstacle Wall' from the previous chapter. Let's imagine your challenges are bricks in that wall. Self-destructive feelings and patterns of behaviour are the cement holding the bricks in place. Fear, resentment, anger, doubts and guilt only strengthen the cement, so everything is held even more firmly. It is this which prevents you moving past your obstacle. It is *that cement* that you need to let go of.

Unhelpful feelings, thought-patterns and beliefs are the very things that give your challenges the power to keep you stuck and pushing on the wall. Letting them go is the greater challenge because if you reject or push them away too forcefully, all you end up doing is giving more of yourself.

Picture it this way, you're pushing against the wall, you're using everything you have to push harder. You want to knock it down so much that your whole being becomes consumed. This is not letting go in its true sense, nor in the right way. This type of resistance only firms up the cement between your bricks, holding challenges firmly in place, attaching limiting beliefs and negative patterns of behaviour to them. This makes it harder for light and solutions to find their way through to you. Instead of letting these limiting factors build your wall higher, see them, acknowledge them then lay them down beside your wall. Use them to deconstruct the wall you've built around yourself as self-defence. The things you should be letting go of are the very things holding your wall in place. Ego might stop you from asking for help, self-doubt will prevent you from believing in your own ability, guilt will lock you in a cycle of feeling bad, expectations (your own and that of others) will keep you doing what you've always done to please everyone but yourself. None of these things will help you break-through the wall. Give yourself permission to weaken rather than strengthen the cement, find a way to chisel it out from between your bricks, remove your obstacles one by one.

AND MORE EFFORT...
Just because we've let go of something in the past, doesn't mean it is completely resolved. True healing (the result of consistent letting go) takes much deeper work. There are layers developed over a lifetime of building beliefs and repeated behaviour. To fully heal from a challenge, we need opportunities to let go at deeper and deeper levels. If you do this consistently, in time you'll succeed, your challenge will pass.

Let Go Of The Things That Hurt -Things That Aren't Good
One type of letting go involves acknowledging and releasing those things in your life that are hurting you. This requires you to be deeply honest about the negativity surrounding you, whether it's people, places, jobs, limiting beliefs and especially our own behaviours. Give yourself permission to walk away from anything damaging. Then, you can start filling that space with things that give you positive energy. No one can lift you out of

negativity except yourself. Your wellbeing depends on you letting go of what has hurt or is hurting you. By doing this one thing you will see miraculous changes in your life.

Let Go of Other People's Expectations

One of the most self-limiting behaviours that so many of us share is the ego-based need to please. We live our lives trying to impress others or be something we're not. By letting go of this desire you are effectively granting yourself freedom to just be yourself. The less concerned you are with what others think, the more you can be true to yourself and live your life according to your truth. A deep sense of inner peace and fulfilment will follow.

Let Go of Your Own Expectations

As one of the world's most inspiring thought leaders, Wayne Dyer, put it, "Peace is the result of retraining your mind to process life as it is rather than as you think it should be". Do your best, nothing more and nothing less. *That* is all you should expect from yourself, you can't do more than that! By consistently doing your best you can rest assured and feel proud. This will counteract your self-limiting beliefs and your need to live up to your own expectations as well as those of others, because you'll know deep within that you've done the best you can.

Let Go of The Need To Control
Stop resisting what's going on in your life and release it, accept the way it is, accept the way it isn't, and move forward. As soon as you release that need for control you'll let go of negative energy and bring in the positive.

Let Go of Expectations - expect nothing and then everything you get will be a gift.

Let Go of Blame - yourself and others.

Let Go of Guilt - forgive.

Let Go of The Things That Hurt - negativity.

Let Go of Control - allow issues and events to unfold, trusting that things will work out.

Let Go of Fear - "If we doubted our fears instead of doubting our dreams, imagine how much in life we would accomplish".

~ **Joel Brown**

Let Go of Ego - thinking you know best and can always do things better than anyone else puts you under added pressure to be perfect. Here are

15 Things You Should Let Go Of To Be Happy

- Let go of your need to always be right.
- Let go of your need for control.
- Let go of blame.
- Let go of self-defeating talk.
- Let go of limiting beliefs.
- Let go of complaining.
- Let go of criticising.
- Let go of the need to impress others.
- Let go of your resistance to change.
- Let go of labels.
- Let go of fears.
- Let go of excuses.
- Let go of the past.
- Let go of attachment.
- Let go of living life to meet other people's expectations.

EXAMPLE:
You've decided to throw a party! So many of your friends have been stressed lately, everyone has been so busy with work and life

that no one has connected in a long time – a party is the perfect excuse to gather everyone together, let your collective hair down and spend some quality time reconnecting. You've taken action - taken the bull by the horns and want to give everyone a party to remember! You're buzzing with excitement and it's all planned, down to the last detail. A perfect party - electrifying atmosphere, lots of people, fabulous food, music pumping, everyone dancing, drinks flowing, everyone partying hard.

You've been counting down the days, but when the party finally happens it doesn't happen the way you expected. There are lots of people, but they aren't dancing like they're supposed to, instead they're sitting in groups, scattered round the living room, lounging about, chilling, chatting and having some deep conversations.

There *is* music, but not dance music it's mellow, chill-out music. The food IS delicious, drinks *are* flowing but there's a calm, peaceful atmosphere with a steady murmur of conversation and soft laughter.

It's not at all how you expected it to be and you end up spending the whole night frustrated and irritable. You wanted it to be just how you'd pictured it, you can't let go and just enjoy.

Truth is, it was the perfect party - everyone had a fabulous time, no one wanted to leave, your guests were able to connect on a deep and meaningful level, relax after a stressful week and everyone felt replenished and energised - except you - you spent the night frustrated, agitated and disappointed.

IF only you were able to let go, even just a little - of your expectations, your eagerness to completely control things, your need for things to be perfect, your frustration that they weren't - you would have been able to open up to see what was really going on. You would have been able to enjoy the moment for what it was, recognising the underlying vibe you were aiming for was indeed created. It was an unforgettable party that left your friends feeling restored, de-stressed and wanting more, it unfolded as it needed to, to benefit everyone there.

This example provides the perfect analogy for the concept of letting go, while still taking responsibility. It's a hard balance to get right but so powerful when you do. If you hadn't taken responsibility to throw the party in the first place it wouldn't have happened. You need to hold onto your dreams and desires, take responsibility and actively make them happen at the same time as finding a way to let go and allow things to unfold as they need to. The universe knows your deepest desires and intentions and if you can trust those will be met, you can be more present in the moment, knowing you've done everything you could whilst accepting the universe will provide circumstances to meet your deepest desires, your heart's intention, your ultimate purpose for doing and being.

And letting go is an integral part of the process . . .

Chapter 5

E

Enjoy The Process

Choose to see your life as an adventure, embrace it and all that comes with it.

"Life is a journey not a deslination."

This chapter brings us full circle.

Although it's time to focus on the last letter of The SMILE System™, *the 'E'*, this powerful principle contains within it the entire SMILE System. It pulls together all the insights and lessons we've learned so far, connecting them to one another in a way that helps us see the big picture of life and understand the true purpose of the challenges we face.

Let me explain . . .

The 'E' of The SMILE System™ stands for: **<u>ENJOY THE PROCESS</u>**. *It relates to:*

~ The '**<u>S</u>**', how you **<u>SEE</u>** your challenges and obstacles. Ultimately, if you choose to see things differently by adopting the **perspective** that your life is a process *(your process)*, then you'll *know* that everything you're going through is in fact, taking place to benefit you in the long run. This is an incredibly empowering way to live! You'll no longer be a victim, instead, you can make the most of every challenge that you face, learning from each of them as part of your growth process.

- Viewing your life as a process, enhances your ability to **MASTER YOUR MIND SET** (the '**M**') by providing you with an immediate **thought shifter**, a tool to help you change gear in your mind. Think about it for a second . . . when something goes horribly wrong, it's so easy to get sucked into the vacuum of reactivity and lose the plot. It's easy to think the worst and only natural to try and resist or run from the threat of change. BUT, by seeing what you're going through as part of your process it pulls you out of your head. It's forward thinking. It shifts your focus from thought (the dialogue inside your head) allowing you to take action in the moment and proactively make the changes you need, to improve your situation.

- Knowing that your life is a process, carries with it so much promise - the **promise** of an **INSPIRED** life (connecting you to the '**I**') - A life filled with potential, hopes, dreams and possibilities. So, the more inspired you can be by who you are, by what you're working towards and especially about the challenges you face, the more powerful this final principle can be for you.

~ And, this all-encompassing concept will ultimately help you with the '**L**' too because, seeing your life as a process gives you the **freedom to allow things to unfold** as they need, so you can in turn **LET GO** of what you need to. When done in a balanced, responsible, proactive way this gives you an uplifting, empowering way to live.

Let's explore the 'E' in more detail…

Do you ever find yourself stuck, in the middle of a crisis or dilemma, feeling immense pressure and wondering – "Why is this happening to me? What have I done to deserve this?" A time when things feel so upside-down and messed-up that you can't make sense of how you've ended up in such a state, with things so bad you can't see a way out?

This final step of The SMILE System™: ENJOYING THE PROCESS will show you how to turn what seems like an insurmountable obstacle into something beneficial and empowering so it can serve you.

You see, when you're in the thick of it, when you're in the pain of a situation and feel broken and hopeless, you are actually in the most powerful place to be – you're '*IN PROCESS*'.

Think of it like this . . . when you bake a cake or cook a delicious stew, all the ingredients get thrown in and stirred up. At that stage, the cold, wet ingredients are an unappetising mess. It's only when you turn up the heat and leave it to cook, that the messy mixture is transformed into a mouth-watering masterpiece. Without the heat and pressure of the cooking process, no transformation takes place, and a messy assortment of ingredients that could be so much more, never quite gets there. The heat and pressure is a vital part of the cooking process . . . It's where the magic happens.

Our lives are the same!

Circumstances change, situations beyond our control have a way of throwing us off course, and before we know it we're mixed-up and confused. We lose our sense of self and feel broken and out of control. Somehow this creates more pressure internally, as unease grows and expands, and externally, from our relationships and environment which seem to add fire to the furnace in response to our unravelling.

But the truth is, in the heat of the situation, in our moments of pain, when the pressure is at its most intense, we have the greatest opportunity to redefine ourselves.

The pressure created by external circumstances acts as a catalyst, leaving us no option but to change and adapt. And if, in that moment of extreme pressure, we're willing to be completely open and honest with ourselves, we have a powerful window of opportunity to truly 'see' ourselves and identify our personal 'garbage' with clarity. Only then will we be able to shift things, to truly heal and evolve.

Throughout life we are being transformed by experiences, taught by our challenges and trained by the obstacles we face, to become the best version of ourselves.

You are a work in progress and the life you lead is your process.

So, the question to ask yourself is: *Who am I in the process of becoming?*

Think of your life as a road map. Where you are now, the circumstances surrounding you with the issues and challenges you currently face, is your starting point. The person you aspire to be: all the things you want to accomplish, your hopes, dreams, goals and aspirations, is your destination.

And, as with any road map, there are a whole host of possible routes you could take to reach your destination. The choices you make, as you journey through life will lead you down various paths. These are effectively the streets, roads and motorways of your life map.

Some choices will result in extraordinary life-changing experiences, others might lead to what appears to be a dead end. At times you'll feel you're on the road to nowhere and at other times you might feel stuck in traffic, frustrated that you don't seem to be moving. And then when you finally reach your desired destination you'll often find it's not what you expected it to be at all . . .

You've done it! You're there! You've finally arrived! But when you look around at what you desperately wanted you somehow still feel empty. So, you set your sights on a new destination that you reckon will fulfil you, and your journey continues.

The truth is your whole life is a journey. Everything you've experienced along the way, is part of your journey and has contributed towards making you who you are today. Everything you are yet to experience will contribute towards moulding you into an even better version of yourself - the person you have the potential to become. All the bumps in the road build you. The way you respond defines you. Your challenges are the bumps you turn into building blocks. You are a work in progress and your life experiences, both good and the bad, are part of your process.

The fulfilment you seek, the happiness you desire, isn't necessarily contained within any particular goal, however much you may think it is. It's more about the journey than the final destination so it's the journey itself that should be enjoyed. Think of it this way; the experiences you gather along the way, the people you meet, the wisdoms you uncover and the connections you make, contain within them their own sprinkling of joy and always add value to your life, making all the difference when you eventually get to where you're going.

True fulfilment lies in the work of getting there, the journey, the process of building the life you dream of. Reaching your final destination will be incredible of course, but without appreciating what you've achieved along the way, without being conscious of your process, you'll miss out on so much.

Having goals is essential and you need a clear picture of your desired destination - after all you can't expect to get where you're going if you don't know where it is! It's important to know what you're working towards and carry this vision with you. The secret here is to remember to savour the journey as much *or even more* than the destination. True fulfilment, the joy and sense of achievement we believe we'll attain when we get to that end point, can be enjoyed just as much along the way with this perspective. And remember, things change, and if you're doing it right, you'll be evolving and transforming too, as will your end goal.

To turn your obstacles around and uncover *how* your challenges can serve you, you need to be clear about who you are. You need to be clear who you aspire to be and what you think is standing in your way. Clarity on this will let you understand what your challenges are teaching.

Remember in Chapter 2, when I asked you to create your 'I AM' Statement – *this* is why we did that! Let's revisit it now . . .

I'm certain, by the time you've reached this chapter you've already grown and evolved a great deal, you can't have reached this point without transforming in some way. Revisit your I AM Statement - incorporate all the things you now know about yourself, all the lessons and insights you've gathered as you've progressed through this book. Think about who you're becoming.

Once that's done, I'd like you to take a minute to answer this one very powerful question for yourself...

How are your challenges helping you become that person?

If **MONEY** (or lack of) is your challenge, why do you think you are going through this challenge? How is it part of your process? Is it to help you appreciate what you have, to learn how to budget, to work harder for something or is it for another reason?

If your area of challenge lies in **RELATIONSHIPS,** could your situation help you learn about self-worth or the meaning of a healthy relationship?

Is your **WORK** stress there to grow your desire for something more meaningful or to push you towards creating balance in your life?

If you're **TOO TIRED** to do what you need to do or to make changes you want, look at how you spend your time and what it is exactly that's draining your energy.

During SMILE coaching sessions I work through this powerful activity with my clients, using the mind map/spider diagram technique we used in Chapter 1 to create your life map.

You can do this for yourself now, in one of two ways:

Either pick one challenge on which to focus and place it in a bubble in the middle, OR (*preferably*) write your name in the middle and dot your challenges in surrounding bubbles.

- **MAIN FOCUS** – <u>MONEY</u> (in the middle)
- **MORE GENERAL FOCUS** – <u>YOU</u> (in the middle) with challenges around you.

Success Tip

You can use this technique to reflect on why you're going through what you are, and to figure out how each of your challenges are there to support your process.

This will help you respond to situations and circumstances in an empowering and beneficial way.

Next, think about *(and jot down)* how that one challenge in the middle OR each of the challenges in the bubbles can serve you. What are they there to teach you? Write whatever comes to mind dotted around the page. Then, draw a line from the challenge, leading to the various growth opportunities each offers.

For example, if you now know your money challenges are there to change the way you view or look after your finances, you can take steps to improve the situation. If your relationship hassles are there to help you learn about self-worth, you can work on building your self-confidence. If work stress is pushing you towards a better work-life balance you can schedule some time out. If you are exhausted with no energy, you can do something that inspires you and boosts your energy.

By knowing why things are unfolding as they are, you can take responsibility for making the changes you need.

As the centre of your own universe, as the sun in your own solar system, things *do not* happen to you, they happen *for* you, so it's time to start responding to challenges and obstacles in that way!

Trust The Process – "What's meant to be will always find a way."

Feel excited about working and transforming towards something or somewhere greater.
We're all striving for something more - happiness, fulfilment, meaningful relationships, more money, better jobs, improved health, the list goes on, so why not enjoy the journey? By injecting excitement into everything you do you automatically become a positive creator rather than a victim of circumstances.

There is a stunning explanation that I want to share with you that explains this insight exquisitely. I believe it originates from the teachings of the grandson of one of the greatest thought leaders and mystics from the 17th Century called The Baal Shem Tov. He said, **When we feel like we have fallen and we don't know how to get up, when we can't seem to find our way or don't know where to go and everything seems wrong, when nothing seems to be working or right, at those moments, we have to go anyway, try anyway, because eventually a universal truth will be revealed - everything happens for a reason, we had**

to go through that process, AND we will actually learn that we NEVER FELL, nothing really bad happened, and it was all part of a bigger plan.

How empowering is that?!

Seeing your life as a process allows you to live in the now, be present and deal with the process whilst still holding on to the inspiration and promise of the future.

No challenge that you're facing is insurmountable.

All too often we get so caught up in wanting the end result that we don't embrace the process. Living a happy, fulfilled and successful life is more about a journey than the end result. The real rewards like building strength are found in the process.

Trust in the Process.

A talented friend of mine wrote an exquisite poem that expresses the point I'm making with beauty and sensitivity. Simon and I volunteered together at a children's educational charity, called Spirituality for

Kids, many years ago and spent the most amazing year coaching at-risk teenagers from deprived backgrounds in life skills, spirituality and personal growth. Simon is one of the most genuine, generous and inspiring people I know. His own life has been full of challenges.

Simon was born in a tough part of West London, on the outskirts of three notorious council estates, to a single teenage mother. His father was a married man in his twenties. Being of mixed race came with additional complications in the 1970's. Simon barely had a relationship with his father's family but received a lot of love from his mother's. Things were tough for his mum from which he learned lots of valuable lessons, vowing never to do the things that upset him as a child. Unfortunately at the age of 12 he lost faith in both God and life and started doing the things he'd vowed never to do; he became involved in crime, took drugs and abused alcohol, he caused chaos and at 15 was kicked out of home as he refused to change. He was in trouble with the police, left school before taking his exams and at that time was expecting his first son. That relationship didn't last and another son was on the way with a different partner only 6 months apart. At 17, as a father of two baby boys, Simon became desperate to make a change. He longed to be the positive role model he'd craved as a child. Through a bizarre route he found his first mentor at aged 18, an inspirational music producer who taught young offenders to turn their lives around. He even allowed Simon on his course with a baby as he was a single parent at the time (and would be, on and off for the next 13 years of his life). This had a most positive and profound impact on Simon's entire life. For 3 years, until his untimely death, his mentor showed him values and principles he could take and use to shape his future: to serve others unconditionally; to be hard working; to be a loving parent and partner and; to always be respectful and creative. Simon has used these skills in his personal life and to help others in a range of areas including the music and entertainment industry, teaching and personal development fields, financial planning and business consultancy over the past 25 years. To date, Simon has helped to impact many thousands of lives, and his goal is to continue doing that for as long as he can.

I'm honoured that Simon has given me permission to share his beautiful poem with you. It's called: *On Reflection:*

ON REFLECTION

Today I awoke, with a new refined me. I'll speak straight from the heart, on reflection, honestly. I've held back in my past, why such procrastination. When my life is a journey not a simple destination.

I've walked and fell down, like when a child takes those first steps. Been in love, broken down, had a thousand regrets. Yet I always survived, I'm alive, by G-d's grace.

Through the tough times and great times, I give thanks and embrace.

The life I've been gifted, that so many have shared. My teachers and mentors, that made me prepared. To love and be loved, that's our deepest connection. As I assess my whole life, I feel blessed on reflection.

A poem by Simon Wilcox
20/11/12

Choose to see your life as an adventure, embrace it and all that comes with it.

Taking this a step further, have you considered, it's only *after* going through a challenge, that the reason it needed to happen becomes clear?

This next activity helps you identify, reflect on and appreciate the lessons learned and growth experienced from *previous* challenges.

ACTIVITY 10

TIMELINE – LESSONS FROM THE PAST

Let's explore what your challenges are there to do for you by looking at what your past has taught you?

1. Grab a blank sheet of paper.

2. Write *'LIFE IS A PROCESS'* in a bubble in the centre.

3. Pick 3 challenges you've already overcome.

4. Write these challenges in their own bubbles around the central bubble.

5. Leading from these challenge bubbles, write down the answer/s to the following *questions:

   a) How did this challenge help or improve things for you?
   b) What do you know about yourself now that you didn't know before each challenge?

(check out the sentence starters in the Success Tips box)

Success Tip

Sentence starters to help you with STEP 5:

This challenge helped me …

_____

This challenge improved things for me by …

_____

This challenged showed me that I …

_____

Thanks to this challenge I now know that …

_____

ACTIVITY 11
FOCUS ON THE FUTURE

When facing new challenges:

- Find what you can learn from them.
- Why are they happening for you?
- How do they serve your process?

Let these words inspire you…

"When you fight through difficulties, you reveal your greatness. And since we have all had to fight through challenges at some point in our lives, we all have greatness inside of us. The measure of one's greatness is found in the size of the challenges overcome. No challenge you are facing is insurmountable. It's a universal law that you will never receive something you can't handle, or something that won't ultimately bring you more happiness in the long run. You just have to trust it. It's easy to get caught up in wanting the end result instead of embracing the process. Sometimes we are in such a hurry to reach the finish line that we forget about the importance of the journey. Success is not the end result. The real rewards like building strength are found in the process. Trust the process"

Yehuda Berg

This final practice of The SMILE System™ is the simplest and most profound of all.

You can now use the gift of hindsight with foresight and face new challenges, armed with the wisdom gifted to you from your own past experiences, coming from a place of strength and positivity, knowing that after the challenge, when you come through the other side, the reasons why, will become clear.

"Let me fall if I must fall.
The one I will become will catch me"

~ The Baal Shem Tov ~

CONCLUSION

You started learning The SMILE System™ all those chapters ago, to empower you in some way. Perhaps you'd been feeling stuck or overwhelmed and wanted to explore new ways to view and deal with life's challenges. Maybe you were searching for something to help you lead a happier more fulfilled life. Whatever your reasons for being here, I'm so pleased you are.

The measure of your determination for self-growth and self-improvement will make all the difference to your success in life - and the fact you're reading this now, shows what you're made of - and you are inspiring!

The SMILE System™ has changed my life in so many ways. It's changed how I cope with adversity and given me the tools, inspiration and strength I need to live life the way I want to, according to my own dreams and aspirations, and, above all, it has made it possible for me to carry within me a deep sense of who I am and who I aspire to be.

I know it will do the same for you, maybe even more, because you now have these same tools to support you. You've heard some powerful insights that I hope have raised your awareness and inspired you. You've learned some incredible techniques to use as you grow and evolve into the person you have the potential to become.

Life is a continuous journey and, whether we like it or not, there will be bumps in the road.

You will face challenges (it's inevitable), there will be potholes to circumnavigate and bridges to cross. At some point you'll feel stuck in a traffic jam, getting nowhere in a hurry, and at other times you'll feel as if you're being swept along at great speed, pulled down the freeway of life. But it's the bumps, potholes, bridges, traffic jams and hectic times that build us, they are all part of the process, the Grand Design.

AND YOU CAN DO IT! You can become that person. Hell! You ARE BECOMING that person. The universe is making sure of it.

In the last chapter and throughout this book,

I've talked a lot about life as a journey or process. It's also often compared to a game. But we're never told how to play it, exactly what the rules are or what winning means. Have you ever thought, "Why doesn't life came with an instruction manual?"

That's what The SMILE System™ can be for you, your instruction manual to help and empower you. There is no secret formula for winning, but there is a universal wisdom that once understood and embraced, can contribute towards building meaningful relationships with ourselves and others, in all areas of life. The SMILE System™ helps you access this wisdom within yourself.

Whilst researching some of the deeper psychological concepts within this framework and looking for inspirational resources to share, I came across Cherie Carter-Scott's **'10 Rules for Being Human'** created in the mid-1970's for a training programme she was running. You might have come across them on the internet; they've been circulated via email in the past, posted on pretty much all of the social media platforms and even printed in brochures. These words of wisdom have even been published in Jack Canfield and

Mark Victor Hansen's legendary book, '*Chicken Soup for the Soul*'.

Cherie's 10 Rules are inspiring and resonate so powerfully for me. They complement the lessons and practices that make up The SMILE System™ in the most perfect way, so I'd like to share them with you now *(with some of my own insights and comments thrown in for good measure of course.)*

If Life Is A Game Then These Are The Rules:

The Ten Rules For Being Human

By: Chérie Carter-Scott. PH.D.

Rule One:
You will receive a body. You may love it or hate it, but it will be yours for the duration of your life on Earth. Make peace with your body, accept its imperfections, look after it and respect what your body needs to run at its best.

Rule Two:
You will be presented with lessons. You are enrolled in a full-time, informal school called "life". Each day you will have the opportunity to learn lessons. Your lessons will be unique to you. Be open to them and choose actions that align with your true path and with who you aspire to be. Remember, as we said in the 'S' of The SMILE System™, SEE THINGS DIFFERENTLY, seek the lessons in every situation.

Rule Three:
There are no mistakes, only lessons. Growth is a process of experimentation, a series of trials, errors and occasional victories, so its inevitable things won't always go to plan or turn out how you want. The failed experiments are as much a part of the process as the ones that work. View mistakes as opportunities to learn. Be compassionate, learn to forgive, live your life ethically and keep a sense of humour.

Rule Four:
The lesson is repeated until learned. Do you find yourself repeating the same patterns in life? Learn to recognize those patterns and the lessons they offer. Problems, challenges, irritations and frustrations are more lessons and they will be repeated for you in various forms, until you've learned them. Once you've learned one lesson, you can move on to the next. Your own awareness and ability to change are requisites to successfully moving passed each lesson. Another fundamental aspect is taking responsibility – take your place at the centre of your own universe and accept that you are not a victim of fate or circumstance.

Be empowered to grow beyond your challenges.

Rule Five:
Learning does not end. There is no part of life that does not contain lessons. While you are alive, there are always lessons to be learned. Embrace your role as a student. Commit to the process of constant learning and change - be humble enough to acknowledge your own weaknesses, and flexible enough to adapt as you need to, because rigidity will deny you so many new possibilities.

Rule Six:
"There" is no better than "Here".
Be grateful for and enjoy what you have right now, along with where you are on your journey. Appreciate the abundance of what's good in your life. The grass isn't always greener over there. In fact, more often than not, when you get to wherever 'there' is, you'll find yourself searching for another 'there' that looks better than where you are at that point. Live in the present to find inner peace. Dance the fine line between living in the here and now while holding your dreams and aspirations safe in your heart, for the future.

Rule Seven:
Others are only mirrors of you. You cannot love or hate something about another person unless it reflects something you love or hate about yourself. Be tolerant; accept others as they are, strive for the clarity of self-awareness; have an objective perception of your own self, your thoughts and feelings. Negative experiences are opportunities to heal wounds you carry. Support others, and by doing so you support yourself.

Rule Eight:
What you make of your life is up to you. Every person creates his or her own reality. You have all the tools and resources you need. What you do with them is up to you. Imagine yourself at 90, looking back, what would you want to see? Embrace all that you are and all that you're not.

Rule Nine:
Your answers lie inside. Trust your instincts and innermost feelings. Listen to the soft voice of your kinder self, and look for flashes of inspiration. Draw on your natural inspiration to guide you. Look, Listen, and Trust, all you need, lies within you now.

Rule Ten:
You will forget all this at birth. Somewhere along your journey from the spiritual world to the physical one, you forgot these rules. But they are universal truths that lie within each and every one of us and can be called upon whenever you need them. So, live your life with consciousness and awareness and let these rules support you on your journey.

Isn't it amazing? Even though we've come to what seems like the end it's really only the beginning . . .

We've been through the entire SMILE System framework and you now know that:

SEEING your life as a process empowers you! It helps you **MASTER YOUR MINDSET**. It **INSPIRES YOU** to push through your challenges and frees you to **LET GO** of the what you need to. So make the most of your process, **ENJOY IT** along with your challenges, obstacles and struggles, they are all a vital PART OF YOUR **PROCESS**!

You've invested in this book and originally set out to learn The SMILE System™ because you wanted to discover how to stay positive through life's ups and downs. And I hope I've inspired you to shine your light on the world, no matter what you're going through and that this book has served you well. I hope you've picked up some new insights, tons of tips, tools and techniques to empower you along the way.

There is one last thing I'd like to mention before signing off - something for you to think about beyond this programme . . .

I don't know about you, but there has always been something about the words 'POSITIVE' *and* 'POSITIVITY' that has niggled me for some reason. It's not the words themselves that bothered me, more how over-used these words have become. POSITIVITY and POSITIVE THINKING are terms bandied about all over the place. They're used and sometimes abused in so many different contexts that I'm not even going to begin to list them. I can't help but feel, along the way, they've somehow lost their meaning and more tragically lost integrity and authenticity. Which is a real shame, because isn't

POSITIVITY such a powerfully charged word?

Several years ago, when I gave my first ever SMILE talk, the feelings of unease and resistance I picked up from other people when I mentioned I was giving a talk about positive thinking, made me question what I was doing. But rather than give up completely, I decided to take the bull by the horns and investigate what this charged and over-used word really means, especially in the context of how we live our lives. So, I searched where any self-respecting, aspiring luminary of the 21st Century searches - I went to Google, or rather to The Oxford English Dictionary and other definitions on Google, and was encouraged and fascinated to learn the dictionary definition of POSITIVE is as follows: *(I've picked 10 definitions that really resonated for me but there were tons more):*

POSITIVE OR POSITIVITY IS:
1. Characterized by or expressing certainty or affirmation
2. Tending to emphasize what is good or laudable; that it is constructive.
3. Very sure; and confident.

4. Moving forward or in a direction of increase or progress.
5. *Biology:* indicating movement or growth towards a particular stimulus.
6. *Medicine:* beneficial or satisfactory.
7. Completely certain.
8. Believing that good things will happen or that a situation will get better.
9. **Adjective**: Showing a situation is likely to improve.
10. **Verb**: Doing something to try to improve a situation rather than doing nothing.

Well, who can knock that? POSITIVITY is definitely worth going for! It was after checking out these definitions, that I thought HELL YES! The skills and practices contained within The SMILE System™ programme will empower everyone who uses them to turn things around by awakening the positivity within.

Do you know what? I am the luckiest person I know. I've had my fair share of challenges. I have had to work through some really tough things. I haven't always had it easy and I have had to dig really, really deep to find my inner resources to pull me through. Life has provided me with a plethora of challenges to learn from and experiences for growth. My journey has been filled with ups and many downs. I have cried tears of frustration at our bleak financial situation. I have felt challenged beyond what I thought I could handle. I have had my heart broken, my dreams shattered and have had to pull myself back from the brink of despair, several times along the way. My certainty and belief in myself have been put to the test many, many times. The pressure has sometimes been so overwhelming. And do you know what; I wouldn't change these experiences for the world!

It's because of these challenges and obstacles that I am who I am today. Each and every struggle I have faced, each and every bump in the road that's thrown me off track, every single hurdle I've had to overcome, has taught me something about myself and the world around me I'd never have learned without them. And I wouldn't change them for the world.

And the same goes for you. The world is your oyster! You have incredible power to create the life of your dreams, in spite of what you're going through right now. I hope you can see that? Hell, you're the centre of your own universe! You can be whoever and whatever you choose.

I hope you'll use The SMILE System™ to support you as you grow and evolve and that you ENJOY THE PROCESS you're going through as you become the person you have the potential to be, the person you aspire to be. I hope you feel empowered, excited and inspired to live your life to the full.

I hope you'll SMILE your way through whatever challenges you're facing, now and in the future, and that you'll call up your own inner tools to help you make the most of every situation. You now have the resources and awareness to connect to your inner strength and find a deep sense of peace and fulfilment that no external circumstances can touch.

YOU ARE AN INSPIRATION!
I believe in you!
So, Go out there!
Believe in yourself!
Live your life!
& Shine!

Ronit xxx

The SMILE System™ Core Skills

S = See Things Differently

How you see things has the single greatest impact on how you experience them... So, from now on seek and see the opportunities in every situation. Transform challenges into gifts by using them to your advantage, knowing if you overcome them, you can overcome anything. Every obstacle you stumble across, every single challenge life throws at you, is actually nothing more than an opportunity to grow, learn, develop and above all transform. By 'Seeing Things Differently' you'll be turning your challenges and obstacles into something completely different, something positive. Your challenges will become your portal to something better.

M = Mastering Your Mind-Set

Your thoughts have an incredible impact on the way you live your life, because ultimately your actions are governed by your feelings and your feelings are influenced by your thoughts. By 'Mastering Your Mind-Set' you'll be far better equipped to manage the way you mentally process what's happening around you and as a result, own how you deal with events and emotions.

I = Inspire Yourself

Inspiration is the fuel that drives us forward. It connects us to our inner creativity and lights the way to out-of-the-box problem-solving. Think about how alive and driven you feel when something inspires or excites you. By choosing to 'Get Inspired' you'll be re-igniting that feeling when you need it the most, energising your powerful emotional propeller, and that can't help but move things forward. Inspiration is the bridge between feeling stuck and taking action.

L = Let Go

We hold on to so many things in life, even when we know they aren't doing us any good - emotional baggage, hurtful relationships, destructive behaviours and past physical injuries or health issues. All of these can take up disproportionate space in our lives and stand in the way of happiness. Releasing that hold isn't easy, but finding a way to let go, means you're clearing a space for positivity to move in. Freeing yourself from whatever is holding you back, allows you to see and choose exactly what's needed to move forward.

E = Enjoy the Process

Everything in your life is there to serve you. All obstacles and challenges are for your benefit as you grow and transform. Seeing life's challenges as an integral part of your learning process, knowing you can overcome them and come through stronger immediately puts you in a better place. I'm not suggesting you greet every hitch with open arms but, without past challenges you wouldn't be who you are today. And without your current challenges you won't become the person you have the potential to be. Enjoy the process of becoming a better you.

Ronit Gerber is an experienced educator, motivational speaker, coach, therapist and businesswoman. In her thriving complementary therapy clinic, she personally combines the ancient art of reflexology with motivational coaching, to promote healing of body and mind. She has also brought together, an ever-growing group of therapists under one roof, all specialists in their own field, providing an exceptionally comprehensive range of services to clients. Her commercial background includes her role as Staff Trainer at Selfridges & Co. In past educational roles, she was Lead Teacher for an educational charity and Head Teacher of a Religion School. Ronit is passionate about personal growth and continually inspired by human potential.

The SMILE System™, Ronit's unique personal development programme, is available internationally as a coaching and audio programme, inspiring people to make the most of their challenges and their lives.

Ronit has delivered talks all over the world, sharing powerful messages with thousands of people, from entrepreneurs to corporate professionals, from complementary therapists to women's groups and teenagers alike. Ronit is a regular guest on BBC Three Counties Radio, co-presented a talk show on VIBE Radio, Watford and is the presenter of The Creative Herts Show for 21CTV.

With her enormous enthusiasm, Ronit brings insight, energy and warmth, not only to her YouTube channel, (RoniTV) and popular blog, but to every aspect of any project she undertakes. Her dream is to make The SMILE System™ accessible to millions of people around the world and this book is just the start of making that a reality.

Become A SMILE System Certified Coach

Would you like to add a powerful, effective coaching tool to your toolkit?

Would your clients benefit from straightforward, easily applicable techniques to help them find their inner strength and move forward?

Have you considered training as a SMILE Coach?

Incorporating The SMILE System™ into your coaching or therapy practice will be transformative for your clients. It will inspire them to see themselves, their lives and their challenges in a new and empowering way that will positively impact all areas of life.

Why train as a SMILE Coach?

The SMILE System™ will enhance the way you work with anyone who needs to shift their thinking and view their challenges in a positive, proactive, forward-thinking way.

As a certified SMILE System coach, you will learn how to guide your clients through one of the simplest personal development programmes in our industry.

Complete with:

- tried and tested worksheets
- inspiring stories and anecdotes
- powerful activities
- reflective exercises and
- ongoing support (via The SMILE Association)

You'll have everything you need to coach your clients in this life-enhancing coaching programme.

Whether your goal is to forge ahead in your business or you simply need to add something special to your offering...

**JOIN OUR TEAM
OF SMILE COACHES**
to take your coaching practice
to the next level:

"I believe that The SMILE System™ is a gift to the world. After having learned and applied The SMILE System™ in depth, on a personal level and with clients in my practice, I feel that due to its many layers, it is appropriate and gettable for anyone, at any stage of personal growth."

Lisa M, *Life & Consciousness Coach*

"I found The SMILE System™ to be exceptionally beneficial and unique as a coaching tool/system. The strength of the system is that it allows one to examine one's life as a whole - it is not about facilitating a total life "overhaul" but about acknowledging one's strengths and areas of success in life. It also allows a refreshing look at "problems" as rather being opportunities to do and see things differently."

Stacey L, *Physiotherapist*

Contact Ronit
Website: www.ronitgerber.com
Email: info@ronitgerber.com

Printed in Great Britain
by Amazon